Feminine Hues

(Short Stories)

By

M. C. Williams

ISBN: 1-4107-5772-2 (Electronic)
ISBN: 1-4107-5771-4 (Paperback)

Library of Congress Control Number: 2003093869

This book is printed on acid free paper.

Printed in the United States of America
Bloomington, IN

1stBooks – rev. 05/30/03

GOES AROUND, COMES AROUND

Oh, it is nice to be black and single. People usually don't appreciate their circumstances until they are over. Not I. I appreciate my lonely nights, my peace and quiet, and not being responsible for another human being. It is hard sometimes when you hear a bump in the night and there is no one to protect you. Sometimes, you wish there was someone, just one person in the world that understood you completely. Eventually, you would get tired of that person because he would never argue with you, he'd just say, "I understand you, dear." That person would take all the fun out of living and the relationship would die. Personally, I'd rather just snuggle up with a good book sometimes. No disappointments and no back talk. I go to movie theatres alone, restaurants and amusement parks. Sometimes, I meet people or just bask in the solitude. I'm not celibate but I am selective. I am because not everyone is special enough to taste my wares or to experience the height of ecstasy.

All of my girlfriends are married or have bastard children. I can't see myself in either situation. Maybe I'm just selfish. Selfish to the bone. I have come very close to the whole thing, marriage and children. I chickened out. The thought of giving up pieces of myself and my freedom gave me the shivers. I remember telling a friend of mine, "I thought I was selling my soul to the devil." She was flabbergasted at my nerve to walk out of the church and into the abortion clinic. I thought I had more nerve to be in a holy place wearing white and pregnant in the first place. I could list a billion reasons why I thought I did the right thing but why list them? I have no regrets.

Secretly, I know my girlfriends envy me. They want to be able to go out anytime they want. Unfortunately, the little man and the whaling brats hold them back. I always hear, "Not this time Renay. Maybe next time when I can get a baby sitter," or something like that. I see the look of desire in their eyes. When I visit, I often see the dull look of being trapped in a routine. It is just as well; at least they are taking responsibility for their actions. There is nothing worse than seeing a woman running around all of the time when they have a husband and children at home. Pathetic. Anyway, I've stopped asking them to do fun things and have reserved time to go shopping with the little mothers and wives. They hate my sarcasm because they know that I am not kidding when I say, "did you ask if you could go out?"

My mother loves my lifestyle. She likes to see me with nothing. She wants to keep her youth and grandchildren would just kill her. She wouldn't be a good grandmother unless she was disabled and even then I wonder. My selfishness comes directly from my mother. She had me out of wedlock and probably would never have married if it wasn't for that. Abortions were unheard of then, I think. Or maybe she was fearful of the Lord. Many lives have been ruined behind her thought processes. Herself, a man, a few other children, and me. Those are the breaks, cookie. Anyhow, my lifestyle is directly influenced by the ability to rub my freedom in her face. I am single and happy. She is married and unhappy. I have no intentions of joining the bandwagon.

I went to college and finished just to have something else to hold over her. She never finished. I got my driver's license when I turned 18; she never got pass the permit stage and is still struggling. I bought my own home straight out of college. I own my own business, drive two nice cars, and travel extensively. Like on jeopardy, "Things my mother will never do in her lifetime? Correct Ms. Wilson. You have just won $10,000 for that answer."

I always ask myself, "Why am I the way I am?" I wonder if I am doing the right thing. I think too much fun is sinful. I must be very sinful. I like to have wonderful experiences but will not indulge in them for too long. I like depravity. I enjoy depriving myself and others to teach someone a lesson. I think that is noble. I also believe that if you don't leave at the right time, what was once wonderful can become very sad. I learn from my mistakes. I used to try to drag things on because I remembered the fun in them, only later did I realize that what I was holding on to was a memory. I move through life like I move through a hotel; you leave your baggage at the door, rush to the new face at the counter, take what they have to offer (which is the key to the beginning of something new), then quickly move on before the thrill dies and you feel over charged.

I thought I was the only person in the world who held this philosophy about life until I met Raoul from Cape Verde. Raoul Gorba. The first thing that attracted me to him was his serious appearance. I like men who seem authoritative and in control. He was sitting by himself at the bar outside near the pool at the hotel drinking a perfect martini. He seemed rather romantic sitting in the dark drinking in the dim glow of the waning moon. I noticed him when I first walked in. I was attracted to his foreign appeal and his nice brown skin. He was wearing the native garb but something about him seemed rather Americanized. Maybe it was the martini with the olive in it. I ordered a Pina Colada. I sipped and gazed in the heat of the African night. The next drink he asked for in his perfect Spanish accent was a Pina Colada and that let me know that he was aware of my presence and interested. He finished his drink, left money on the bar, and walked to my stool. "My wife, she doesn't understand me," he whispered in my ear as he rubbed against me.

"Then maybe you should explain yourself to her better," I whispered back as I slowly sipped my drink. I had met his kind before. They like to throw lines at you just to get your reaction. He was not trying to share his life with me and he wasn't interested in getting his life story off his chest. He wanted pure unadulterated sex. He was not going to ruffle my feathers with that one.

"I'm not married."

"Neither am I, Mr…"

"Raoul Gorba, Ms…?"

"Wilson," was all I said with a smile because I didn't want to get too personal. I wanted to tease him and I could sense that he wanted a challenge and a good one. He had the right woman.

"Well, Ms. Wilson, what brings you to my little island off the coast of Africa? Men? Business?"

"Yes." I had a few lines myself so I hit him with a one. "I need someone to show me around the island. You look trust worthy. Besides, you are a native aren't you?" I looked innocent, but he read right through me.

"A bright and intelligent woman like you looks more than capable of finding her way around. Are you saying you are intimidated by strangers? You should never have left your country alone and you certainly shouldn't be speaking to me. But from looking at you, you seem very comfortable and secure here by your lonesome." I could smell his body odor. It was pleasingly strong.

"You have mastered the English language, Raoul. Have you been to the States?"

"I went to college there. I lived in the United States when I was younger and was homesick. There is no place like home, Ms. Wilson."

"Renay. So, will you take me up on my offer? You know, show me around during the day. I'll pay all expenses."

"No nights?" He laughed and I liked it. It was strong. "It just so happens that I am on vacation.

5

What kind of man would I be to take money from a woman? You just take care of yourself. How long are you here?"

"Indefinitely. It all depends on the natives." I smiled at him. I noticed that he had light brown eyes and they smiled back at me.

As we left the bar to get some dinner at a local restaurant, I was wondering about the character of my Latin-African friend. He was rather quiet on our way to the restaurant. I began to compare him to other men I dated. I rather liked his silence. It was better than the over exaggerated chatter of the Frenchman who escorted me up and down les rues de Paris. His silence was more comforting than the insecure Spaniard who kept asking me if I was having fun in Spain. Senor Gorba was secure enough with himself that silence was refreshing for the both of us. The restaurant that we entered was crowded and it unnerved me for a little while. I had a sip of my marguerita and was able to people watch. I was amused with the crowd. Some people were speaking French, others Spanish, and still others in an African dialect. The restaurant was named El Norte and served North African cuisine. Raoul and I commenced to speak Spanish and he was impressed with my fluency.

"Why are you attracted to me?" He asked out of the blue. He sincerely wanted an honest answer. His eyes bore through my soul and I decided that sarcasm was not appropriate.

"You are attractive; you are a foreigner. I am a modern day explorer. I would like to climb your peaks and sample your merchandise. I like adventure and you are my adventure."

"Let me first correct you. You are the foreigner here. You are a poetic little wench. I don't know if I like you. You are too aggressive. You have hunger in your eyes. People don't mean anything to you, especially, men but since you are able to be honest with me I will be honest with you. I, too, would like to sleep with you. Once you have conquered me, we never have to see each other again. I am sure that is your usual routine. Only a stupid man or a man on a suicide mission would take you on. You know too much." He took his shot of whisky quickly. He was looking at me out of the corner of his eyes. Strong words, but he was unsure of my reaction. Either he blew it or he was on to something. Right away, I felt as if he was challenging me, daring me to take a thrill and try to live off of it. The only things that move me are memories when they are good ones. I forget everything else. He wanted to attack me because he knew I would eventually attack him. Maybe he didn't know. Maybe he was hoping I would want more. After the sex, he would pretend he didn't know me just to prove how strong he is. I thought about his offer. Could he make me feel?

"You don't have to like me, you poor bastard. The only thing I feel for you is physical and I can always move on to bigger and better things. I have looked around this place. I have seen the men here. Sure, they don't have your appeal nor are they as intuitive as you are, but they would certainly be better entertainment," I snarled in his native tongue. I calmly finished my last bite of dinner, drank my port and left my portion of the bill on the table along with a generous tip. I got up to leave, but he grabbed the back of my thigh. His fingers were gripping my inner thigh and I stopped in my tracks. He pulled me closer and rubbed his head in my groin. He looked up at me.

"Tomorrow at six, meet me at the bar at the hotel, and I will give you a tour of my village." He looked as if he hated me with a passion. I pried his fingers from my flesh and sashayed to El Casa Amarillo where I was staying. The bastard allowed me to leave alone. If he were some brother from around the way, I would have cursed his mixed up ass out! He was lucky that I was a rather civilized sister. Most of us don't take any guff from anyone and I was no exception. I was the worst sort because I knew how to get you when you least expected it. I don't make scenes either. Usually, I am polite about extracting sexual favors from men, but I don't like beating around the bush for too long either. Foreigners! Had he been a regular brother from Long Island, he would have been pleased with my advances and there wouldn't have been a scene. Did he think he could tame me? I hate men who think they are invincible. Men who think they are in control. I especially like to see that type lose control.

I did not realize then that I was dealing with a man much like myself. We treat people the same. He knew me before I realized who he was. We try to out wit our prey. He had his hang ups about sex and male-female relationships as well as I did. We had gone through similar struggles but we refused to share our past with each for a long time. Raoul became one of the few steady men in my life. We were together for a long time, but never discussed the other relationships we had. Our relationship was based on the here and now, that is, once our relationship got off the ground. When we first met, it was six feet deep.

When I got to the hotel, I thought about calling my mother to rub my exciting vacation in her face, but decided that I couldn't fake it. My life wasn't all that exciting at the moment. Raoul had done something to me. I would call and she would know that I was unhappy. I changed my clothes and took a stroll on the beach outside the veranda. I went back to the bar and flirted with the bartender a little. He was cute and would probably be a good roll in the hay, but decided against it because I would have to see him every time I came down to get a drink afterwards. It would spoil my vacation. I must admit that being single on a vacation where everything is so romantic is definitely one of my hang-ups about being single.

The next morning I decided to make the best of it and maybe I would find a one-night stand later in the evening. I took a car to town and told the driver to drop me off on the busiest street. Sightseeing would take my mind off of my loneliness. It was funny how I didn't realize that I was lonely until after my scene with Raoul. I strolled up and down the street looking in shop windows and amusing myself with trinkets. I decided to stop in a bread shop for a bun and a drink. The men looked rather nice, but I would not be happy until I defeated Raoul (not knowing that my own destruction awaited me). Maybe then I would be able to move on and enjoy myself. I had no way of reaching him and there is no way in hell that I would try. If he contacted me then I would be agreeable. Enough of him. I made up my mind to contact some of my old college buddies who were native Cape

Verdians. I visit them every time I take a trip to Africa. I decided to call in the evening and arrange to stay with them. Raoul was a lost cause. I called a cab to take me back to the hotel. When I got to my room, there were African violets in a vase with a note attached.

"You, too, are a rare beauty. I must see you. I desire you." There was a number but, no name. I wondered if it was Raoul or the cute bartender. I then realized that I was supposed to meet Raoul at the bar at six. It had totally slipped my mind. I called my friends and arranged to stay with them for a few days. I watched a few movies and arranged to go on a boat ride. I would call the number on the flowers in the morning. As I was lying in the bed, I began to wonder why Mr. Gorba was at the hotel bar if he lives on the island. He wasn't a very nice person. I'm glad I didn't meet him today. I certainly didn't really need him for anything, I already knew my way around the island. I would like a little company, but I could get that from anyone. I feel asleep with the television on.

I was just waking up when I heard a loud wrap at the door. I swung the door open expecting it to be one of the maids. It was Raoul. "Well, well," I mumbled, "did you come here to ruin my day?"

"Quite the contrary, I came to brighten your morning. Did you receive my gift of violets?" He came close to me and ran his fingers through my hair. He was breathing on my cheek.

"Rather expensive gift for a woman you don't know. Or maybe you were rather lonely and would like to buy my company after speaking to me so harshly." I stepped away from him and proceeded towards the bathroom to freshen up. Someone knocked on the door and he went to answer it. I did not like the way he was making himself at home.

"Breakfast has arrived." I heard dishes clank together and bottles opening. He was trying to make things pleasant for me but I was just going to ruin it. I walked into the dining area where he was seated and stood by the chair that I was supposed to sit in. He got up to pull it out for me but I refused to sit down. He went back to his end of the table and I stared at him.

"What are you doing here?"

"To apologize for my rude behavior. I let you get to me."

"You are a little too late. Besides, who wants to dine with a liar?"

"What did I lie about?" He cut into his omelet and continued to eat.

"You said that you were a native, but if you were you wouldn't be living in a hotel."

"I would if I had a spat with my girlfriend who chose to kick me out of my own apartment," his hands were shaking as he shoved more egg into his mouth. He chewed slowly and swallowed hard. He was feeling the pressure of my stare and banged his fist on the table.

"Damn, bitch. Fucking around with my best friend. My fraternity brother at that. Although, I can say that I never genuinely loved her, I would never sleep with any of her friends. At least, she could have had enough respect for me to tell me that she was interested in sleeping with him. I would have given her time to pack her bags and find a place to stay. She decides to fuck him in my bed; I walk into the room

11

and there they are. It was so unexpected. I walked up to my friend and said, "hello." I sat on the couch and turned on the television. I asked Michelle were was dinner. She jumped out of the bed and started throwing my model cars at me. She said I was uncaring and unfeeling. What does she know? She hated me and never wanted to see me again. I gathered my things and left. This happened the day I met you. I sat at the bar all day uninterrupted until you came along.

"Sorry to have disrupted your beautiful day," I smiled at his suffering. I sat down and we ate the remainder of the breakfast in silence. I noticed his widow's peak, his nice straight hair, and his lean upper body. He had nice rather delicate hands. I imagined that he was a skilled lover. He looked at his watch.

"Please hurry Ms. Wilson. We will miss the boat if you are not ready by nine o'clock." He said it rather nonchalantly, but he had perked up a bit. I sprang from my chair and rushed to get ready. I was going to have fun, I could tell.

Raoul grabbed me by the waist and looked into my eyes, "You look delicious, Renay."

The boat ride went around the island of Cape Verde. The food was very ethnic and so were the drinks. I got very drunk, but it added to my enjoyment of the festivities. There was a lot of singing and dancing and a whole host of party games. I met a lot of interesting people and was amazed at my nonsexual interest in the men. My senses were consumed with Raoul Gorba. I didn't have a desire for anyone else and that is unusual for me. I watched him play, mingle, and entertain. He introduced me to everyone he knew and he made me feel special. It was getting very late and I was getting tired. Raoul noticed me yawn and excused us from the crowd. He took me to the upper deck where there were sleeping cabins.

"This is an over night trip, Renay," he whispered as he removed my clothing. He kissed me delicately all over my body. He put me to bed and tucked me in. I feel fast asleep.

When I woke up he was lying naked next to me. I ran my hands over his body. I stared at him for a while. I kissed his cheek and got out of the bed. I got a hotel robe and sat in the chair by the window looking out onto the beach. I don't know how long I was sitting there when I heard Raoul singing softly behind me.

"I must leave you today to visit friends in the country," I whispered expecting him to be upset by the news.

"Okay, darling. The boat goes back to the port at noon. It's nine o'clock now. Let's hurry to breakfast before they close the kitchen."

We showered together without making love. I could not understand his lack of desire for me, but correlated it to his lingering affection for Michelle. I understood but my sexual desires were reaching its peak. I did not want to rush him but I wanted him. What was he trying to do anyway? He wasn't treating me like an object and that is what you do when the only thing you are after is sex. He was turning this into something more and I don't think I like it. He was washing me and I was trying to figure out how to tell him that this was too much. He must have sensed what I was thinking and feeling.

"You know Renay, I am very attracted to you. I wanted to make love to you last night, but I want it to be good for both of us. I think if we get to know each other better we learn more about our sexual selves; therefore, our lovemaking will be pleasurable."

"That is nice in theory, but don't you think you will be creating a situation by us getting so familiar with each other. I'm not trying to marry you." Or even know you, I thought to myself. I don't like having feelings attached to a memory. I just want to think about the sex and move on. All ready I was feeling something. I thought about what he said though. I guess it wouldn't hurt if he knew what I liked. I asked him if he learned anything about me yet.

"You like your lovemaking slow and you don't like to feel attached to the person you are having sex with."

I grinned. I like an intelligent man. A man who studies the woman he wants to make love to. Most men don't take the time and I hate to say it, but most Black men don't take the time. A woman will stumble on one or two men educated in "Womenology." For some reason though, we never marry that man. I think because we know he has seen so many women that one woman is not special to him; his desire is to try them all. He will only truly be happy with the woman who denies him. He will follow her to the end of the earth. I am not that type of woman. If I like you, I want you but then, get lost. I have my limits. Refusing sex from a desirable man is not part of my thought processes. I will be single for the rest of my life.

"Can I ask you to do me a big favor?"

"Sure, you can ask Raoul."

"Please do not sleep with anyone until you have slept with me." I looked at him and laughed. He was very serious and a little hurt.

"You are asking a lot. Besides, I don't see the point in that. What are we waiting for?" This man was strange. He definitely had me intrigued, but where he was going with this was a mystery to me.

"Please. It would mean a lot to me."

I kept laughing but agreed. We spent most of the morning chatting about my friends and his girlfriend. I asked him what he was going to do about her.

"I don't know. What do you suggest?"

"Communication is the best solution. That's what I hear anyway. I think you unnerved her with your inability to vocalize your feelings, if any. Eventually, women know when men fall out of love with them. Michelle found out before you realized she did. That is why you were shocked to see her with another man. It didn't matter if it was your buddy because you didn't love her anymore. You were shocked because you thought she didn't know. She became infuriated with your accepting attitude because it confirmed her suspicion. You don't love her anymore. She may never forgive you, but I think you need to talk to her and at least tell her why especially, if you want to get your stuff back. How long would you have continued in a loveless relationship?"

He thought about what I said and agreed that he needed to talk to Michelle. He said he would never have left her. I thought that was odd.

"You mean to tell me that even though you no longer love Michelle, you would have continued to go through the motions?"

"You would be surprised at how many men do."

"If that is the case, then why not patch things up and go back?" I did not understand men and I wasn't really going to try. I knew what I knew about them and I used it to my advantage. I didn't need to know this. He shrugged his shoulders in response to my question.

We made it back to the hotel at twelve thirty. I called my friends to let them know I was on my way. I couldn't wait to visit Grace and Markus Ansez. I had gone to college with Grace and met her husband when he used to visit her there. They always seemed rather happy together until I arrived at their home. Markus barely said a word to me and Grace was in tears. I had just walked in the door and dropped my bags. I looked around at them and retrieved my bags and immediately apologized for my intrusion and turned around to leave. I had never been in the mist of their falling-outs. I was embarrassed to even be there and believed that it was best that I leave.

"Please stay," Grace begged by back as I was almost out the door and was looking to see if the taxi was still visible. It was. Grace shut the door. She went to sit on the loveseat and Markus was sitting in and armchair. I picked up my bags again and went to sit next to Grace. I did not want to discuss what had happened between them so I asked about the kids, work and their health. Everything I asked about was fine.

"We are getting a divorce."

I said nothing. I wanted to leave. I did not want to hear the reasons behind their big decision. I was starting to believe that if there could be a good marriage, theirs was it. I was always wrong about these things. Sure, I saw them have vicious arguments, but they always made up. They have been together for so long that I thought it was permanent but I should know better. I felt that the end of their marriage was the beginning of the end of something within myself. It was strange. Even now when I look back, I realize that my feelings were all too accurate. It made me realize that most stable things (people) eventually, go through change no matter how hard they fight against it. I, too, was changing.

Grace began to tell me how Markus was having a slew of affairs. I started fidgeting because I didn't want to be one of them. I really didn't want to stay. He interrupted her to tell me that he told her numerous times that they should go to counseling.

"Counseling? Counseling? Markus, I think we are mature enough to handle our own problems without an interpreter that will cost us a fortune?"

"We've been discussing our problem for years and I am still unhappy Grace." He got up to get a drink. The house was silent. I was becoming curious about their marital situation and asked the lovebirds a rather personal question.

"Grace isn't satisfying you sexually, Markus?"

"No, she isn't." He was just as blunt.

"Why not Grace? Too busy?"

"Renay, you know what it's like trying to hold down a job and keep your man happy at the same. In addition, I have children." Yes, I could sympathize. I took the chicken's way out—no husband and no children.

"I have offered to hire babysitters, take them to mothers, and even to get a nanny. Grace refuses. She loves the children more than she loves me. She says that she still loves me, but her actions speak differently," explained Markus.

"I think that you both need a vacation. I also believe that you need counseling and more time to just sit down and talk. I am puzzled that Markus's adulterous behavior did not anger you. Are you having an affair Grace? I mean, do you still love your husband?"

She did not answer me. I understood her silence and excused myself. I took a walk along their beach and thought about relationships. I reminisced about my old relationship with John. It was a long time since I had thought about him and the baby I almost had. I wondered what it was like to be married and have children. I wondered if I was missing anything. Would I ever fall in love? Real love? I was twenty-seven and had a lot to look forward to. I wondered what was going to happen to Grace and Markus. I wondered what Mr. Raoul Gorba was doing. I was feeling rather sexual, but I remembered my promise and I laughed out loud. It was ridiculous of me to make such a promise to a stranger but I did want to make love to him and wanted it to be tantalizing. I decided that it was in my best interest to comply.

The Ansez's usually have a lot of visitors on the beach during the summer but this summer, I noticed that only their relatives were there. I spotted Markus's brother Noel just as he spotted me. We had had an affair a long time ago but nothing much came of it. He was always very attractive to me and I always wanted to have sex with him. Not this time. He was too big. I mean I was beginning to detest his large physique. His heavy body on top of mines would suck the life out of me. I wanted a little man. I wanted Raoul. All of my past men were on the large side because I thought bigger was better. I guess when a person grows up, they get a more mature view of life. Anyway, I started flirting with Noel just to distract myself from the seriousness of the atmosphere in the Ansez's house.

"Ah, the most lovely woman in the world, Ms. Wilson," he was grinning very broadly.

"Ah, the biggest liar this side of the island," I said with a grin.

"Not true! I may be the most honest man you know," he replied in his defense. "And you look as if you need a drink."

"How true."

I had a neat scotch while Noel looked me over. I intentionally refused to return his gaze. He nibbled on my ear and I giggled as I moved away.

"What is this all about? You never avoid my advances. Is there a man in your life, finally?" He sounded genuinely astonished.

"There is always a man in my life. I would rather take a ride on the motor boat and go fishing, that's all."

"Well, let's go," he said as he shrugged his shoulders.

On the way to the docks, we met up with a few other guests. We all got into the boat and set off for the middle of the ocean. The company was rather entertaining. Grace's second cousin Dina and her fiance Guillome, Grace's childhood friend Minerva, and Markus's Uncle Georges all accompanied Noel and me. As we sat with our hooks below water and a glass of scotch in our hands, we began talking about business. I had met everyone before and remembered what he or she did for a living. When we got tired of talking about ourselves, we discussed what was going on with other entrepreneurs like ourselves. Minerva started talking about new Real Estate tycoons, which was right down my line. We both were into real estate in one form or other. I owned a lot of various properties and she sold them.

"Did you know some gentleman is planning to invest a few million dollars in condominiums on our very island? He is one of us you know, a native, but he travels back and forth to America. These condos, he says, will be for lower class Cape Verdians. He is going to tear down the old apartment buildings and replace them with an upper class look."

"Really? I believe that could improve living conditions, but how does he plan to make money like that, is the question." Georges asked in disbelief to anyone who cared to answer.

"Maybe he has a good plan, uncle," answered Noel who doesn't know much about real estate.

"Plan or no plan, he will lose money if he is unable to make a profit," Georges shouted.

"He says he is going to give the people a chance to own something in order to build their credit to buy a home of their own one day. They will be able to sell the condominium as if it were a house," commented Minerva.

"Yes, yes, I know all of that but how is the man going to get money from people who can't get loans," yelled Georges in exaggerated disbelief.

"Pipe down old man, you are scaring the fish," remarked Guillome who was a serious fisher.

"Georges poses a good question," I stated in this defense. "How will he be able to support himself if this project fails?"

"He's a millionaire. He will find other ways of rebuilding his capital. It is good to put your neck out for a cause rather than pure profit," said Noel.

"What's this guy's name?" asked Dina.

"I don't remember, but I know he has other real estate investments that are working rather efficiently for him," said Minerva. "I read about him in yesterday's paper under Real Estate."

"Weren't you mentioning that fellow to me yesterday Guillome?"

"Yes, Dina. I believe his name is Gorba. Raoul Gorba."

I choked on my scotch. Noel patted me on the back rather roughly. He was such a brute. "Are you okay?"

"Yes." It never failed. I always met some fellow who is semi-famous or some kind of international tycoon on my trips. Most times, I wouldn't find out until I left the country. It was better that way.

"Do you know Senor Gorba, Renay?" Minerva now had moved closer to me to hear whatever gossip I had to tell.

"Not really. I am familiar with that name."

"You should be. You both are into Real Estate. You probably heard some lawyer or other mention his name. I believe he owns a lot of property in America," explained Dina. "Isn't that right dear?" She was talking to Guillome as he is reeling in a fish; the first catch of the day.

"Wow, that's a big one!" Noel had reverted his attention to Guillome and so did the rest of the party. Everyone got quiet and began fishing. I was pretending to fish while my mind was racing. Had I heard Raoul's name before? In America? Gorba? I did not recall any major projects done by any Raoul Gorba. I wanted to ask more about the article but decided I would investigate the matter on my own.

My first thought was millionaire? Mr. Gorba is a millionaire. Then I eased off that thought. I was wealthy so it wasn't the fact that he was a millionaire that surprised me it was just that he didn't act or dress like one. As I began to reflect on the boat trip, I realized that he seemed to know a lot of people. Then, I remember the African Violets he bought me; those flowers are very rare. It must have cost him a small fortune. That was enough proof for me. My problem now is how do I act towards him? Pretend, I don't know? I definitely can't continue to treat him like the peasant I thought he was, can I? Well, why not, I thought? He's just a man. Why was I even giving this any thought? I just wanted to have sex with him. Unfortunately, this wasn't taking the usual course. Usually, I would have had sex already and I would be arranging other convenient times to meet. I wouldn't have spent time talking to him and telling him my plans for the day. I certainly wouldn't have promised not to sleep with anyone else.

We went back to the dock rather late, three in the morning. I caught four fish. The total on the boat was thirty fish. Some of us did better in grasping the fish while trying to unhook him; others let a few slip back into the water. We competed with each other with the size of the fish and the skill in reeling them in. Georges was extremely inebriated and so was Dina. Most of the way back to the dock, they sang a cappella.

I went to the beach house Grace had prepared for me. There were a few notes on my nightstand. One was from Grace asking me to spend the day with her. The second was from Raoul asking me to remember not to forget what I promised, however, he hopes I have a good time. I smiled and climbed in the bed.

I woke that morning to the maid knocking on the door. She wanted to clean the room and tell me that Grace was waiting for me. I washed quickly and got dressed. I spoke to some of the other guests who were already out sun bathing. I went up to the big house hoping Grace had some breakfast prepared. To get to the house from the guest beach houses, one had to climb about one hundred stairs up a hill. Once up the hill, all you can see is a path that looks as if it goes through a forest. It is Grace's garden that she cultivated herself with native horticulture. After the two minute walk through the garden, one comes to the back of the house where there is an ocean blue pool underneath a portico which seems redundant with the ocean just at the foot of the hill. All that you can see beyond the pool is glass. Glass that spreads from left to right and meets the garden on both ends. I walked around the pool where Bathsheba and Simba, their rottweilers, were sitting quietly. I slide the glass doors back and rang for the butler. It would take too long for me to go scouting around the house for them. Grace came to greet me.

"I knew it was you." She was very happy to see me.

We hugged and I asked her where the servants were. She said she dismissed them all because she became suspicious of them. Only the servants for the guesthouses were still employed. She was the only person home and Minerva and her mother had just left. They stayed with her most of the morning. I asked her if she and Markus spoke any after I left yesterday.

"I want to thank you for listening to us yesterday. I guess we wanted an audience. I decided to agree to counseling and he agreed to spend more time with the children. I need time to get away sometimes. He took them shopping this morning. I want him to know that just because we are wealthy doesn't we aren't responsible for raising our children. They are both of our responsibility."

"There is no way around that. I certainly agree with your point of view. But tell me, are you still in love with him?"

"I truly don't know Renay. I never had an affair but I wanted to. Sometimes, I want to live as you do and I told Mark that."

"I can imagine he wasn't too pleased. Besides, you have children. You aren't willing to risk losing your children just because you fantasize that my life is some big pleasurable adventure. It isn't you know?"

"I never had the chance to experience life as you do so no, I don't know. I have no idea what it is like to be free from commitment and responsibilities. I love my children, but I feel as if my life will be over before I could really enjoy it. I deserve some time to myself."

I understood her desire to be free, but she didn't really know what she was wishing for so I tried to explain it.

"My life is full of responsibilities but not the kind of responsibilities that you have. I am responsible for making sure that I can manage my finances and believe me, that is a task when you are doing it all alone. I spend a lot of time alone. There is no one for me when I am sick. There is no one for me to share silences with. That means something to me. I don't know how to share and I envy that in you. I am out here all alone, Grace. When I die, there won't be any children standing around crying about me or telling stories about me." I wasn't sure if I believed what I said because I hadn't given it much thought before now. I did know for a fact that I was not as happy as she would like to believe.

"Oh, Renay. I am so sorry. I don't think I can live like that. You make your life seem so carefree and easy. I would never have known how it truly was if you didn't tell me."

We walked around the house and she showed me all the new things she had done. Grace has always been a good decorator and it was evident from the way she designed the interior of her home. She had fifteen rooms and seven bathrooms. She had relatives who lived with them, but they were away for the summer or were indulging in the fanfare of living in the beach house. There were a few people still at home and we peeked in on a few people. I had heard the names before either in conversation with Grace or by way of gossip from Dina.

Grace asked me what I wanted to do and I suggested shopping for lingerie. I wanted something nice for myself. She and I went in her car. We talked about old friends and party invitations. She asked me what I thought about Guillome. All I could say was that he was a good fisher and that he seems rather quiet.

"I think he beats on Dina. The first day she got here a noticed a mark on her back. It was black and blue. I asked her about it and she got really embarrassed and defensive."

"I did notice that he grabs her a lot. I mean when he wants something, he grabs her wrist and asks her to get it. I only thought he was just a physical person."

"Too physical if you ask me. Women should marry men smaller than themselves for their own protection."

"You have weird ideas, Grace."

"Maybe, but a man should never hit a woman for any reason. Women aren't even protected by the law. Women need to wise up and protect themselves. Don't you think that if a man hits you once that is an indication that he is abusive?"

"I agree absolutely. I remember one boyfriend hit me and I let him have it. The only thing that kept me from taking his eyesight or crushing his balls was the fact that I did not want to cause a scene with his screaming, honestly. I get vicious when I feel threatened. Sometimes, even verbal abuse from a man throws me off balance. I could probably kill a man."

Grace looked at me. "You don't like men too much, do you?"

"Grace, please. You know me. I haven't met one worth keeping."

"Yeah, I know you like to sleep with men but what about marrying one? You probably can't live with one. He would have to be a total wimp or never at home for the two of you to get along. He could never disrupt your totally organized and controlled life."

"It is 2001. Doesn't every woman want power? Once you get it it is hard to let go. Some things never change and some things are destined to. Look at our continent Africa. Who would have imagined it would have a black president to represent every country instead of all the individual countries with separate rulers. A unified Africa. Maybe one day, I will unify."

"Please, let's not get into politics and I can't even imagine a unified Renay. United with your business, but not much else. I'm not a politics person. Let's stick to something that I know like relationships between men and women."

"Oh, I forgot, you know everything about love and relationships."

"I know what I know," sighs Grace. "I know that you operate like clockwork and you should have met someone interesting by now."

"I'm not sure that I want to know what you know and I am not sure what I'm doing with this gentleman."

"Not sure? Are you talking about this Mr. Gorba that Minerva has been talking about? The guy who called you yesterday? What has gotten you all confused?" She laughed.

"Honestly, I'm not sure if they are one in the same. He doesn't appear to be wealthy. He seems so inconspicuous."

"One can never tell with Cape Verdian men. Many of them grow up poor, but if they get lucky enough to get an American education they can come back here and make millionaires of themselves. They never forget where they came from."

"Sounds as if you know him."

"I have met him a few times. The rich always cross paths on this island."

It took us an hour to get to town, but it felt like twenty minutes because we talked all the way. The city was rather busy. Grace parked her Mercedes at the end of the street so that we could walk the length of the commercial area. Grace and I have a rather strange habit; we feed the poor children that scamper in the streets. We make a day of it. We buy them clothes, too. Grace does it frequently and I make it a habit in every country I visit. I like the rowdy children and Grace likes the quiet shy ones. I feel really terrible when I see children like that. Childhood should be the best time in a kid's life. I started a shelter in various parts of the country. Sometimes, I feel so defeated because there are just so many needy children. The shelter we started in Cape Verde is so crowded. So many orphaned or abandoned children. The ones we pick up off the streets are usually the ones from poor families. A meal and some clothing usually helps them make it through the day. I have a responsibility to take care of the children, that is my passion. Especially, the children right in the good old USA. It is a shame how some children are growing up when our country is so wealthy. I wish I could donate more of my time.

After we pretty much cleared the street of children, we went shopping for ourselves. I took a teenager with me because he said he would help me carry my bags. It was apparent to me that he did not want to go home.

Al-Said helped me pick out a few evening gowns. I would try them on and he would give me his opinion about them. He had an eye for fashion. Even the sales women noticed that he had a talent for matching accessories and picking the right color gown. The boutique manager called him over and offered him a job doing stock. Al-Said came to me excited and told me the great news.

"Stock! Where is the manager?"

Said's smile faded as he pointed in the managers direction. The manager was a fair skinned native who upheld a stance of superiority in his boutique.

"Excuse me sir, but I do not believe you would get the best use of Said by merely having him lift boxes. He should be in sales. I demand that you give him a respectable job or my friend and I will return all of our purchases and we will have all of our friends' stop shopping here. I will even go as far as to write the owner of this establishment to make him aware of the unfair treatment I witnessed here today."

"Senora, I am sure you are correct to assume that he would do well in sales but he is inexperienced, young, and I am sure he doesn't have one suit."

"If those are your only reservations I will call the boy over and we will clear this up right now." I waved to Al-Said and he timidly walked over. He was quite fearful of what was conspiring.

"How old are you?" The manager asked with stern disbelief. He probably assumed that Al-Said would lie.

"Fifteen," answered Said.

"Do you have proof?" The manager now seemed regretful for even offering the child a job.

"Yes, senor. I have working papers. I can bring them to you this evening." Said was beaming with pleasure.

"I believe that Said should be given the chance to prove his ability as the rest of your sales clerks and I will personally make sure that he has a suit." I loved a challenge and I was willing to bet my money on Said.

"This woman has a lot of faith in you. I hope you will be able to repay her." The manager was smiling.

Grace and I spent a small fortune on suits and dresses. The manager was even more enthusiastic about Said. He gave Said employment forms and gave him a fair salary. We took him home to get his work papers. He lived in a mud abode. The house was very small with no rooms. He had a number of family living with him. He explained with excitement to his father about his new job. His father, wanting to assist, handed Said some money to buy a suit. Said was sad when he got to the car. He explained that his father didn't have much money and he did not have a suit or anything suitable to wear. I smiled and told him not to worry.

After our shopping spree and settling matters with the manager, we rode Said back home and he gave his father his money back. His family invited us in. We politely parked the car and sat with the family on a rug in the middle of the floor. We drank canned soda and his family expressed great joy. They needed the extra money that Said would make. I gave Said my address and we left them with big hopes for the future. I told him that I would call the store to make sure he was still working.

"Renay, you should be proud of yourself. You may have changed that boy's life forever. He may be able to pull his whole family out of poverty. Jobs like that are hard to come by even for the middle class."

"It is like this everywhere." We drove back in silence.

My days in the country were very peaceful and restful. I did a lot of business over the phone and mingled with the other guests. We all often traveled together on boat trips and get-togethers given by friends of the Ansez's. On my last night there, Grace gave a party in her mansion and invited most of the island. I wasn't amazed at seeing Raoul, but I was surprised that he looked like a millionaire. He was dressed better than all the men in attendance. He spotted me immediately and slipped through the crowd. He put his arm around my waist when he reached me and introduced himself to everyone. His overpowering presence angered me but his touch soothed me. He took over the conversation and entertained the crowd with his plans to renovate the island. He discussed his travels to other countries and his plan to reconstruct the island after the damage created by the war in 1999. He based his plan on one that was being used in Los Angeles.

"I was very interested in Los Angeles's "New Age Project" because it gave Blacks investment power and creative ideas on how to make an environment conducive to economic growth. There will be a summit in January 2002 for all the brown nations in the world to unite." He was very knowledgeable of the summit and everyone was very interested in attending.

Raoul went to give a gentleman a business card that he had left on his table and I was left talking with a gentleman who was interested in what I did for a living. I was happy to announce that I owned property in America and I was in charge of a fleet of rental properties that consisted of offices and apartments. I also had invested in property around the world.

"You must have a lot of wealth and power in America, Mrs…"

"Renay. Ms. Wilson." I wasn't aware what his intentions were.

"I would like it if you attended our summit. Would it be okay if I got your business card and sent you an invitation?" I agreed and handed him my business card.

I walked away from the crowd to the pool area where there was music playing. I stood with a drink in my hand and swayed to the music. I heard Raoul's footsteps behind me.

"You are behaving rather cold towards me. I thought you would be happy to see me. Did you find someone else to spend time with on this lovely island?"

"You know the answer to that and it doesn't concern you. We are just friends Senor Gorba and that is all I want people to think. It isn't even about sex anymore. I think you have made it hard for me to get even simple pleasure from you."

"It won't be hard. Shall we meet later then? No strings attached?" He didn't even believe what he was saying and I am sure he knew I didn't believe him. There were already strings attached.

"I will meet you at your place."

"Oh, well..."

"No need to explain. I know the story about the apartment and the girlfriend is bogus. I know the player's rules—always have an escape."

"What do you mean, he was smiling.

"If you happened to find yourself uninterested after the sex, you could say that you have decided to get back with your girlfriend, Michelle."

"Beautiful and clever. I never had a doubt." I wanted to say so much more but not here. He didn't even ask me how I knew where he lived. He left me but he didn't do it willingly. I was able to mingle the rest of the night. I left the party at midnight for the hotel. I took a taxi to Paloma Avenida and stopped in front of a white house. I paid the driver and walked up the long walk. The house was large and far back from the lawn. There was neatly trimmed shrubbery and a quiet but pleasant look about the place. There weren't any servants and there was only one car in the driveway. I rang the doorbell that sounded like wind chimes. Raoul came to the door with a silk robe on.

"Sweet heart, mi casa es su casa." He smelled very good. His home was well lit. He had a huge chandelier in the hall and lamps all over the living room; it looked like daytime. He had white leather furniture and white carpeting. He had red throw pillows and mahogany armchairs with red upholstery. I was taken by the fact that his living room was very similar to mine except my furniture was black. He had silver touches all around and I had brass.

He took off my dress and led me to the living room. His robe was off and he had on black silk boxer shorts. I still had on my gold and black mules and my black nylon cat suit. He began to bite my neck and feel my body. He pulled me to the floor. Raoul ran his hands through my nice new hair cut. He kissed my face while massaging my scalp. He stared at my body and into my eyes. He took off his shorts and I saw how perfect his body was shaped. He had a runner's body, lean and strong. I was anxious to have him. Raoul gave me a vibra-ribbed lubricated condom that I happily slide on his erection. He spread my legs and held my thighs tightly as he entered me. The anxiety of awaiting his penetration was overwhelming and I heaved with anticipation. I sighed as he thrust into me. He licked and caressed my breasts while I grabbed his buttocks and moved to meet his thrusts. We stood up for stronger penetration. I placed one foot on his sofa frame and the other solidly on the floor. One hand held on to the arm of the sofa and the other on the headrest. Raoul held on to my waist and proceeded to enter me. I got restless with this position when I realized that he had long endurance. I asked him to get on the floor. I straddled him and rode him until he came. I felt the power of his ejaculation with the trimmer of his scrotum beneath me. He clutched me afterwards with the strength of a dying man.

"You were pleasurable. You have more energy than I do by far. Will you stay here for the rest of your vacation? No commitments and no strings attached. I am all alone here and I would like your company."

"I am afraid that the strings have all ready been attached. I don't want anyone else. I am committed to you—during my vacation."

Raoul laughed. He called the hotel and cancelled my reservations. He went to pick up my bags. He was happy that he would have me for a whole week. We talked and got to know each other very well. I was shocked at my ability to share some of my most intimate thoughts with him. I had never done that before but Raoul made it easy for me. When it was time to leave Cape Verde, I was fearful. I had never felt that way before. I was scared to leave Raoul. I even cried. I had never cried before leaving a country or a man. I was miserable on the plane and miserable when I got home.

Raoul came to see me a few times on Long Island and in North Carolina. Often, we would meet on tropical islands or in Europe. We carried on like this for four years until last month when we met in San Juan. I walked into his hotel room and followed the candle lights into his bedroom. He was lying there naked with soft music playing in the background. He got up off the bed and asked me to dance with him. We danced in the candle light for a while. He poured us both a glass of champagne. I sat on the bed to sip my champagne and Raoul kneeled on the floor in front of me. He reached under the bed and handed me a black box.

"Renay Wilson, you have put sunshine back into my life. I love you because when we get together we understand one another. We never pressure each other but I hope that you do not feel angry with me for asking you to marry me. I know that you love me because you come to see me when I ask you to and you never complain about my habits. Renay, will you marry me?"

"Yes, because you make me happy and I don't have to give up anything to be with you."

When I look back I realize that you always have to give up something for love. Love doesn't exist without sacrifice. Our love and lives were too perfect. We felt blessed by God although, we didn't exactly know the meaning of the word blessed. I know the meaning now. Being blessed is when you survive the worst and still have your faith and your wits about you to continue with your life.

That night Raoul and I made love without any barriers between us. We wanted everything that married life had to offer. We planned everything. How many children we would have and where we would live. We had decided to get married today. One month after he proposed. Unfortunately, I had to return to NY to close a deal and Raoul promised to meet me here in a week. Raoul was going to take a plane to LaGuardia where I was going to pick him up. All day I was worried that Raoul would change his mind like I had done to John. I wished that had happened instead of what actually did.

I got to the airport early and sat right by the window where his plane would land. It was a little after his plane's arrival that I heard a loud crash. I looked out of the window and saw black smoke in the air. Someone screamed before I had registered what had happened in my mind. The next moment was a blur. People started running all around me. I heard ambulances and announcements that I couldn't quite make out. Raoul was nowhere in sight and there was a plane crash outside. A plane crash. A plane crash right outside my window. A plane crash a few minutes before my fiance is expected to arrive. I could not find Raoul. I asked a stewardess what happened. She got annoyed because she said they announced the plane crash and that if I was waiting for someone from that plane I should go directly to the hospital. I was at the hospital front desk for six hours. They had admitted Raoul. He died at 8 p.m.

The next day, I had received a letter from Raoul it was as if he was writing me from the grave. He explained how he had drawn up a will with his lawyers. How he had a bad feeling about flying out but he was anxious to see me. He didn't want to wait to take his own jet because it was being repaired and it could take as long as a week. He dismissed his fears as silly and childish. He signed off, "Love Raoul for eternity." When I read the letter I laughed out loud with hysteria. My life was such a cruel joke. I was being punished for my selfishness. I was unable to have the one person that I was willing to share with. I traveled with the body back to Cape Verde the next day by private jet. Raoul was buried in his yard with a statue above his tombstone. Many of his family members attended the ceremony and expressed great sympathy towards me. A lot of relatives stayed with me in his home on Paloma Avenida. I sat up with his mother and father all night. They talked about Raoul as a child. I cried and I still cry. The only reason I decide to write this story is because that I found out that I am pregnant. I have decided to leave the United States to live in Cape Verde to be by Raoul. He left his home and fortune to me. I have decided to continue his business venture and to fulfill his dreams. I have no regrets. I realize how valuable life is and I want to prove that I have changed by raising my baby with the love that I had for Raoul and his memory.

M. C. Williams

DESPERADA

I was getting dressed for the club. This is pathetic. Another night out on the town looking for a good man. How long will it take for me to realize that I will never meet a good man at a club? How many episodes of booty calls and empty promises? I was getting good too. I can spot a loser in a minute. I can sense the ones who have money, legitimately or otherwise. I knew whom I could use and whom I could string along for months or years. Yes, I am a predator. It works for me because I seem very naive and innocent. They don't know it's a game until they are caught up in it. But it's okay. The ones who get caught up are usually the ones who deserve to be used and destroyed. They are the ones who think they are too slick for me. I love it too. I can see them thinking. "This girl is gullible. I can use her and get her hooked." So I continue to go. Very rarely do I spot a man who is genuinely afraid of me. Those are the ones I date seriously. Those and the ones who can predict my every move. I date those men for years. Right now I am in between relationships. I would rather be in a relationship but good scared mind reading men are scarce.

Recently, I came out of a bad relationship. The man wanted to turn me into a woman with low self-esteem. We fought constantly over my demanding and aggressive ways. I was not going to let him turn me into a woman I wouldn't recognize. It would be a matter of time but I wasn't going to stay with him. I planned my escape. I moved out and he never saw me again. I am good at not leaving a trace. I stayed with him for four years. I like to try to work things out when I am in a relationship because I know me. When I am gone, there is no chance of getting back with me. The same goes when I am angry. If you pissed me off, you can hang it up.

The holidays were approaching fast. I was making a mad dash to secure a mate for the holidays. Last year, I wasn't lucky enough to find anyone who could make it to the stretch. This year, I had my fingers crossed. My girlfriend was ready to go to the club and I headed over to pick her up. She was looking sleazy but I didn't say anything. If she got a man that way that was her prerogative.

"Danny, why do you dress like you are going on a business trip? Granted you pull brothers but what is with the suit?" She was looking at me and sucking her teeth. She thought I was trying to show out or something. I was just comfortable this way and when I dropped my lines to hook a fool; the suit added to my demeanor.

"Look. I'm sorry if I don't have hoochie gear. I just feel fly in my suits okay? I don't question what you wear."

"Of course not. I look good." She has issues.

I sped to the club and saw the line around the building. There were honeys everywhere. And when I say honeys I mean honeys. I like my men honey brown or yellow. Big lips and tight. He has to look like he knows what he's doing and where he's going even if he is a drug dealer. I don't make it a habit to pick them up but they are always attracted to me. One dude said it was because I looked like the type of woman that would fight for her man. I laughed. I will fight my man but not for him.

We got out of the car. Gina spread red lipstick all over her lips. I always ask myself why I couldn't find a better class of sister to hang out with. I guess because she is my cousin and knows my secrets. I don't trust anyone. Her lips are sealed and they better be. We got into it once and she was like, "You look like Satan when you get mad, girl. Where you be hiding that anger?" She didn't know how it was from growing up in a house full of boys and with a mother who resented you because you were smart and pretty. My whole family saw that I was a shining star except my mother. She did everything she could to tear me down. All I have to do is think about that and I could lash out an ass whipping on a woman or a man. Growing up, I would tear the whole house up because I would hold my anger in. My brothers tormented me because I wasn't their father's daughter. My mother tormented me because she hated my real father. My stepfather stayed away from me. I lived my life

41

through school. If it wasn't for that I would have been a criminal. It was a plus that I was intelligent. I could get out of trouble with the blink of an innocent looking eye. Going to college helped me perfect my scam to great heights. On one hand, I was professional and dignified. On the other hand, I would get a player, drug dealer, pretty boy and have him hypnotized with my naughty bedroom tricks and ghetto fabulous chitchat. I made a b-boy feel like a king and out wit him at the same time. Shame on me.

I never wanted to be the wifey type. I had bigger plans. I was going to run a business and travel extensively. I was going to have men all over the country trying to get a hook up or wishing I would marry them. I wanted to be famous in my own right and still keep it real. I wanted young sisters to know that they can do anything. Anything! But I was going to give the shit some class. I don't put up with disrespect from anyone.

Gina and I make our way to the line and brothers are drooling. I don't even care why. I don't start my game until I get into the dimly lit club. I like my shit to be undercover. I was in line ignoring everyone. I was thinking. I spotted a dude checking me hard. I smiled because he was smiling. He was perfect. He was creamy and smooth. He was thinner than my regular but he had straight teeth and curly hair. He was foreign. I was flattered that he was attracted to me. I turned my back and felt him staring at my ass. I would play not interested for a minute or two. I had to watch him first.

We go inside and Gina and I head to the bathroom. One dude grabs her hand. She looks at him but he isn't looking like much. We walk away.

"I saw that Arab looking at you." She touches her hair. She licks her lips in the mirror.

"Yes. Yum, yum." I apply my lipstick for the first time. I brush my hair. I smile at myself.

"You are full of shit." Gina laughs. "How long with this one?"

"I think he is a player. Do you see how fine he is? He even was checking out my ass. Player moves already. He doesn't even try to front."

"You are gonna hurt him?" I nod my head. "Good. I can say one thing for you. A man is a man. You break white ones, black ones, whatever. You are fair with your shit."

I laugh. I am ready now and I hear my song playing. I am a true hip-hop head in a suit that mingles Monday through Friday with white corporate America. I know how to assimilate anywhere.

We bop out of the bathroom. I spot a table and make sure it has a view of the honeys as they come through the door. I take out my fat cigar and light up. A few heads turn. One dude grins at me. He thinks it's cute. One dude gives me the hater look. I throw it right back at him like I would kick his ass if he says something. He gets it and turns around. Punk ass. I see a poppie looking my way. Nice Puerto Rican or Cuban daddy. He smiles and I see them crooked teeth but it looks good on him. Dealer. But he's big bodied and I like that. Lips big and brown. I take a seat and order a Merlot. "Bring the bottle, sweetie." Girl friend rolls her eyes. I smile. Girlies don't phase me at all.

Attitude, no attitude. I could careless. Nothing a woman does will get a reaction from me. I don't even notice women half the time unless they try to strike a conversation. I like to pretend I am the only woman in the world. It works too. Most sisters don't understand my attitude at all. It's like I don't even see them. I speak but I don't attribute a color to them. They are like faceless masses to me. But it isn't just sisters, it is all women. I can be civil but don't expect me to go out of my way to get mad, jealous or to notice you. Disrespect me verbally and I'll cut you with my tongue. I have put some people in their place. Believe me, you really don't want to get my attention. In the club, nothing matters but the brothers.

I puff the cigar and I eyeball the room. My cousin is getting all hyped up.

"Girl I want to dance!" She's dancing in her set to Buster Rhymes.

"Go ask somebody. I'll be right here. You know, I got to get my buzz on." She jumps up. She struts to the middle of the dance floor and dances by herself. I laugh at her. The girl is definitely my cousin. To my surprise the Arab is heading in my direction. My, my. He is bold. We just got here and he is trying to claim a sister. Maybe he came out looking for a sister in particular. I mean there are white girls here. Not this man. He is looking at me. My Merlot arrives. I sip. Damn, he's going to catch me before I get myself together.

He stands behind me. He leans toward my ear and asked me if I want to dance. I explain that my drink just arrived and I would like to drink it before I get on the dance floor. I tell him he can join me or ask me later. He takes a seat. He is smiling. I bob my head to Mos Def's joint. I smile because the man is fine. He moves his chair close.

"So where are you from?" I ask him by leaning close and whispering in his ear.

"New York."

"Me, too. What brings you to North Carolina?"

"I was getting sick of the city."

"Who did you come to the club with?"

"My friend, Alel." He points to Alel who is standing by the bar talking to a white chick. I smile at that. This dude is a rebel. I like that.

"So how old are you?"

"How old do I look?"

"Twenty-five." I am impressed that he would think I was that young. I smile.

"How old are you?" I ask before I tell him how old I am because I begin to thing he is far too young for me.

"I'm twenty-seven." That isn't bad.

"I just had my birthday last week. I am 31." His eyes pop out of his head.

"Really?"

"Yes. Am I too old for you?"

"No, my birthday is next month. I will be 31." His lying ass is smiling. He is willing to say anything to be with me. At least he corrected himself before I found out on my own. I think most Arabs are liars. Most men in general but definitely Arabs. He does get points for telling the truth in the next breath.

A Cuban tune comes on. He takes my hand and I get up without hesitation. I think, this Arab is trying to put the whammy on me. To my surprise, he has rhythm. In the next few minutes, he has me spinning on the dance floor. That is a first. I think that there will be a lot of firsts with him. He spins me around and has his eyes hooked on my ass. He never had a black woman, I sense it. He likes big butts. I smile. He will get ass and some other things that come with the territory. He continues to hold my hands. He pulls me close to him. I put my hands on his waist. He brings his cheek next to my cheek. His skin is soft. We dance to three songs but I know that he feels that he is spending too much time with me and he doesn't want to spend his night with one woman. We go back to the table and Gina is there. He leans over to me and asks me my name. I tell him and pull out a business card. I give him one to write his number one. I didn't notice until later that he didn't have the pen and paper like most players. It wasn't until I reflect back on the night that I realize how smooth he really is. I notice too that he gets bored fast. A good thing is that he knows what he likes and he goes to get it. He was racking up points with me. The only thing that was bothering me was his beauty. See, this man was beautiful. I know there are brothers out there squirming but you have to understand. I am not particular about race or color. I just like what I like. There are some fine brothers, cutie pie Spanish men, and good-looking white men. But this man was beautiful and I never saw anyone like him. I didn't think he was beautiful until he smiled. So it isn't his face. It was his smile with his teeth showing. Like, it lit up my little world.

I dismissed him though without that empty feeling taking over. Ladies know what I mean. That feeling that he is gone forever. There are some brothers that you know you will never see again. I didn't get that feeling. He liked my ass too much and because he never had a black girl he wasn't going to stop until he got one. Like I said, I know my stuff.

The rest of the night he was with Alel and the white girls. I danced with a few cuties but he was the only person who got the digits. I didn't find anyone else interesting. I spotted a few cuties but no one who would fall for the game. Maybe next time.

Just like that I forgot about him. I went to work the next morning when I felt like it. My employees were scattering around. One guy never hides the fact that he isn't working. When I catch him roaming the halls he makes sure he speaks.

"What are you doing, Eric?"

"Um, Miss Lady I was just getting something to eat from the vending machine. I'm going to pick up the mail in a minute."

"Come to my office when you get back."

"All right. I'm not in trouble am I?"

"No. Just come upstairs."

"All right, Miss Lady."

I shake my head. I hate to be mean but I like to make myself clear about what I expect from my employees. Hell, I have a supervisor who wants to know how well I manage my people. If they look bad so do I.

I have twenty messages and my pager starts going off. I check the number. It was an employee with an issue. It didn't help that she worked on the other side of the building. I would have to walk over there and then walk to the other side of the building for my meeting. I get half way through my messages when the office phone rings.

"Hello, TTR. Danielle Mason's office."

"Danielle. It is Anwar. You met me at the club Saturday."

"Yes, I remember." Eric comes in and takes a seat. He has a snicker bar in his hand.

"I would like to take you to lunch."

"Okay. Where?" I am trying to keep the conversation short. Eric doesn't need to know that I have a personal life.

"Chili's at 1pm."

"I'll see you there."

I look at Eric and hang up.

"Eric, I notice that you spend a lot of time roaming the halls. Why is it that every time I get here you are walking somewhere? Don't you have enough work? Do you need to be transferred?"

He swallowed the snickers with difficulty. He was sweating.

"Well, boss lady, it's like this."

I look at him as he goes on with his story.

"I would hate to put you on probation so do me a favor, look busy, and stay in your cubicle."

"I can d-d-do that boss lady."

The phone rings as he heads out of the door.

"Danielle. Is Eric up there?"

"He's on his way down Paul."

"He has a lot of mail down here and John is looking for him." Paul was dependable. As a matter of fact, I let him get away with murder because I like him. He does whatever I ask and he does it well. I never have to tell him twice. When promotions roll around, he always gets one.

"What is Eric doing down there?"

"A lot of nothing. Here he comes; I'll call you later."

"When you get a chance, come up here."

"Okay."

Paul was getting promoted to a better position with a raise. It was Paul, Ernestine and Eric in telecommunications. I was demoting Ernestine and giving Paul her position. She wasn't here yet and it was well after 8 am. Most of my employees are black. I have thirty employees and twelve of them are white. The ones in my building have it bad. They see me every day. The ones that work in different buildings get harassing phone calls and emails but are not blessed in seeing my face every day. My pager went off again. I went to see Tasha before I had my meeting.

When I got over there her computer was acting up. I shut it down and called the help desk. They asked me what was wrong and gave me some helpful advice. I straightened out the problem. While I was doing that, Tasha wanted to remind me of her appraisal coming up. I told her to schedule a meeting with me and her supervisor and then one with her and I following that.

"Any day or time?"

"Yes. The times I'm not available are blocked on my calendar. Wherever you can squeeze yourself in, do so." I looked up from the monitor. Tasha was beaming. Unfortunately, just because she got an appraisal didn't mean she would get a raise. Anyway, I could accommodate her in one aspect.

"I set you up. You shouldn't have any more trouble. If you do while I'm in my meeting, call Jack at the help desk. Here is his direct line. He can help you out."

"Cool."

I pulled my suit jacket down over my hips and headed to my meeting. I had to figure out what I would say to the five people waiting for me to have an answer to their lack of secretarial help. I didn't have an immediate solution but I would think of something. When I got to the conference room, two of the executives were seated.

"Al, Mike and Tony are unable to attend. They have an emergency in the demo room."

"Fine gentlemen. I understand that you don't have a secretary over here and you need one immediately. I can offer Tasha's services on Monday's and Tuesday's and Leslie on Wednesday's and Thursdays. Unfortunately, I don't have anyone available on Fridays." I just couldn't ruin anyone's Friday like that.

"Excellent! I think that would help until you get someone permanent. I have heard very good things about both Leslie and Tasha." I was amused at how he put the white girl's name first but I was just happy that they agreed to my solution.

"I will have you set up tomorrow. Unfortunately, I have meetings all day and one of them happens to be with Tasha and Leslie."

"Excellent." They were happy campers. They shook my hand and I left. Meetings my ass. I had a long lunch date and I needed to make sure Tasha didn't schedule our meeting at that time. I had a feeling that she would. I rushed back to the office. My beeper had been going off the whole time. I knew it was my Supervisor. It was about time for her to check in.

I raced to the office and shut the door. I had to take a breather. I just sat in the chair staring at the wall. I had to finish checking my messages but first, I would call Gloria.

"Hello, Gloria. Did you page me?"

"Yes. How did the meeting go?"

"Fine."

"What did you tell them?"

"I offered them the services of Leslie and Tasha. And Tasha is do for an evaluation."

"So. No one gets a raise until August. It's across the board unless the Evaluation is fewer than 80 points."

"Right." I grit my teeth. No one on my team was getting less than 80. My people deserve raises. I didn't care how many times she would roll her eyes. I wasn't going to slight anyone.

"What is your schedule like today?"

"I have to visit my employees. I have two meetings this afternoon and then I am assigning my new employees passwords."

"Sounds like you have a full day. Keep up the good work."

Yeah, right. I hung up. I could pile the bullshit up high. My work would be done by 12:30. I was going to have a long lunch. I would come back here and stroll around the halls and call it a day. I loved managing.

I pulled up my calendar to see when Tasha scheduled our meeting. Smart girl. It was at 3pm. I scheduled to meet her and Leslie at 4pm to discuss their new responsibilities. After that, my day was done.

Preston strolls in. He is my office mate and he never comes in at 8. His hours are whatever. He says he goes to visit his employees first thing in the morning. I could care less. I usually leave at 3 or 4 pm. He stayed until 5 or 6. The good thing is, I am a fast worker and I can get two days worth of work done in five hours. Some days I take a lunch, some days I don't.

I am hyped up at 12 noon. I sit at my desk trying to remember what Anwar looked like. I hoped he wasn't disappointed when he saw me. I was wearing another suit. This one was more feminine though. When I get to the restaurant, I wait in the lobby for him. I am early.

He shows up and he looks nervous. He has a wide-eyed stare. Maybe I was wide eyed too. Anyway, we sit down and he smiles nervously. I think, the daylight is nothing like the dim club. I wonder if this Arab man is still interested.

"Do I look the same?"

"Yes."

"You don't. Did you get any sleep last night?"

"Not really." The waitress annoys him. He frowns at her.

"I noticed that you gave me your work number. Where do you work, Anwar?"

"Well, I have only been here a month and I work at a convenience store for my friend."

"Oh." Arabs and convenience stores. It's no big deal. If that is what he wants to do.

"Do you like managing at a big company like TTR?"

"Yes but it makes me tired. I never have time for myself." That was a lie but believable. As I sat there, I made a few assumptions about him. He is not comfortable eating out. He is irritated big time by the waitress. He wants to fuck me. This time he is staring at my lips. Today, he isn't smiling and he looks exhausted. He wasn't as beautiful as he was Friday night but he is good looking.

"So where do you live?"

"I live in the country."

"Really? I like the country. I want to be in the country surrounded by palm trees."

"You won't find any of those here. Where do you live?"

"Around the corner." I smirk. I see now why he invites me here. I sip my tea. When the waitress returns, I order a glass of Merlot. He doesn't eat much and neither do I. I wonder if he is financially strapped.

"Do you like working at the convenience store?"

"It is okay. I plan to buy one. I have $50,000 that I saved and I am looking for a store every day."

I was impressed. I wanted to believe him but why would he just come out and tell me that? Did he want to impress me? Did he always mention his money on a first date? Did I look like a gold digger? I wondered.

I don't say anything else. I look at him. He seemed untainted. This was the first time that I noticed that about him. It was as if he didn't have a dishonest bone in his body. He seemed naive. I could be looking in the mirror. I wasn't sure. Was he conning me? Did it matter? I had to make up my mind right away how this relationship would progress. I would definitely have sex with him. I just couldn't decide how soon. I wasn't seeing anyone and I was do for a good wham-bam. I had to decide how long he would hang around too. Since he is new in town and I am probably the first black woman he has come across; I may also be his first piece of ass. That was good. Unfortunately, I knew my good luck wouldn't last because he is very handsome. So I decided that this would just be sex. I wouldn't volunteer too much information and I would make sure we didn't lose perspective. I think in the long run he will appreciate this.

He sips the last of his soup and I devour my salad. We are both quiet and intense. I wonder if he can read my mind. You would be amazed at how many people are actually very accurate with their intuitiveness. Even though, I am good at it, it amazes even me. I forget about that. I don't believe he can. He is now smiling at me.

"I want you to see my apartment. I have a roommate but he is at work."

"I need to get back to work."

"It isn't far."

I look at my watch. I would go but no sex. I agree and follow him to the apartment. Anwar lives in a very nice area. His apartment is nice. We sit on the couch and he plays some music. I look at the art on the wall. I am very attracted to him. He sits next to me and kisses my lips. He goes to the bathroom and gets some Vaseline. He rubs it on my lips.

"It just feels good this way." I agree and we kiss again. His hand is under my suit jacket. He sighs when he feels my breasts. My breasts are not small. He takes one to his lips. I look at him. He looks up at me.

"I am not going to have sex with you." He is right about that.

"Okay. I just want to feel you." And feel me he does. "You have the softest skin I have ever touched." He is amazed. His hand is under my skirt. I am moist. He sighs again. I enjoy hearing his sighs. I imagine what he will do when he gets to feel my sex. I feel like silk and I know what I am doing. I am very sensual and so is he. This will be very good sex if nothing else.

In the beginning of the year, I wanted to be in a relationship. It had been two years since I had a good one. I just couldn't find anyone that I liked. Things would get started and then, fade away. He felt different. He didn't seem very experienced in the player's game. For one, he didn't try to get out of taking me out to eat. Two, he was enjoying kissing my lips. Most players avoid lips for fear of attaching emotions to kissing. He didn't have that fear. He was actually enjoying my taste.

I couldn't stay so I pulled back. I was having more fun than I had in a long time. Kissing is my most favorite sex act. I could kiss for hours. The man was giving me what I wanted. Next was sucking my breast. I would allow a man to suck me for hours. He was going there too. What was going on here? I stared at him for a minute or two. I never do that on the first date—look into someone's eyes. I usually save that for someone I love. I believe the eyes are the doorway into the soul. I keep that door closed. Well, I looked and his brown eyes were smiling and the light came on again. This time his eyes were smiling at me instead of his teeth. Funny how a persons interior parts reveal things about themselves that the outside keeps covered. I liked what I saw because it looked harmless but that could have been part of the game for him. I was almost ready to throw my player's notes out of the window.

Well serious, demanding, and aggressive sister that I am, I escaped from lala land. The fantasy was over. I had work to do and I didn't care if I never saw him again but I knew I would. It was so odd. He had a weird look on his face when I left. I would hate to think that he really could read my mind because I think very mean and devious thoughts especially, when sex is involved. I like sex but I think people put sex before all else in relationships. If I was going to have a relationship with a man sex would be one of my least important concerns. He had to be able to offer me more than a few passionate nights. After leaving him, I thought that sex was all he could offer me. I forgot about him like I did the rest.

I went back to the club with my cousin. We are definitely on the prowl because the guy she was seeing turns out to be a loser.

"Girl, Kevin, is still married." Gina is not happy about that at all. "The girl is trying to get all his money. He can't go out or anything. She called the other night talking about she needs money for the kids. It ruined the whole night for me."

I look at her and I am wondering what she is thinking. All he wants is some ass. But then I think, that is all they all want. Anwar, Kevin and every fucking dog off the chain. Nothing is good about any of it. My situation isn't much different from hers. Anwar isn't going to be mine anymore than Kevin will be hers. Men don't marry women like us. I know too much and she is out scamming. I'm not mother material and she is ghetto fabulous. It's a lonely road ahead for us both. She asks me about the Arab.

"He's just another trick in a different skin. We'll see. He isn't using any of the typical player moves but you know those Arabs, they don't love women. They don't even love their own women. They think that just because they follow Allah that they have the right to do whatever they please."

"Oooohhhhh, so what are you going to do? Girl, you know your shit!" She's all excited because she knows that whatever it is that I plan to do it will be something she can brag about.

"First of all, I'm not going out with him unless he buys me dinner. I know for a fact that he will never want to take me on a real date. He saves that type of shit for white girls. He doesn't give a shit about them either but he will wine and dine them because he thinks that is what he has to do. After I give him the pussy, I am going to completely ignore him like he ain't shit. I'm going to break dates and disappear on him. That fucker is not going to get me caught up. Watch what I tell you girl, he will do back flips for my ass."

"I know he will. I remember that white boy you had all doped up. What was his name, Jim? That fool was crazy. He was ready to put you in a house and all kinds of shit. I want to know what you be doing."

"Fronting like I'm stupid. Girl, I'm player number one. I have more game than Michael Jordan."

"You got dollars too so they never see it coming." She laughs and takes a sip of Corona.

In all honesty, I am looking for the man who does it for me. The man who can take me as I am. I have had a few who were dying to marry me but they didn't have the look I like. That is my problem. I am all about looks and I can admit it. If it wasn't for that I would be hitched now. Hell, I would have been tied down at 18 but my standards are too high. I just don't want to spend the rest of my life gazing at an ugly man. I would want to take my own life every morning. I would probably kill the children. I mean it is hard enough being Black in America. Who wants to add ugly to the equation? So I will continue to suffer alone until my fine Romeo shows up.

We hit the club and it was packed. Men from wall to wall. We look around. I didn't see anything. Two hours pass and only the bozos ask me to dance. I dance with one thinking the fly guys will see that I'm not stuck up. It doesn't work. So I scan the crowd. I guess I will have to be aggressive. There are only two hours left. I don't want to look desperate but I would hate to be stuck with Anwar. I made up my mind that there was definitely no future in him. He was story telling material. A relationship I would tell my friends or daughter about in twenty or twenty-five years.

Gina and I leave the club with numbers but I burn mine in the ash tray in my car.

"No way. I have better luck at the flea market."

"Danny, don't burn them! Give them to me. Especially, the dude in the purple suit. He was fine."

She snuffs out the fire and looks for the paper with his name on it. "Is he David? Or what does this say?"

"It is Brian."

"Cool." She finds it and dusts it off. "I like his butt."

"How do you plan to pull this off? When he sees you he will know it isn't me."

"Doesn't matter. I will talk to him for a month or so. If he likes me over the phone he will be dying to see me, I mean you, again."

"Do what you got to do to get your shit." I couldn't go out like that. I like the brother to decide whether he wants me. I hate rejection. I think my whole life centers around how not to get rejected.

I get home at 3 am and my pager goes off. I am not surprised. Eric leaves a message. His grandmother got ill in the middle of the night and he won't be in to work. I can't sleep because I spend the whole night trying to figure out who I can get to cover for him for the day.

I am groggy when I get up to go to work. I get in late on Wednesdays because I have management meetings but this Wednesday the meeting was cancelled. I spend most of the morning finding a replacement for Eric and in the afternoon I rest my head on the desk and take a nap. I wake up when my office mate comes in. I look at my pager. I have ten messages. I check my voicemail. Everyone is wordy and boring. Message number four is from Anwar. I honestly didn't think about him anymore so when he called, I was shocked. He invited me to lunch again. I figured he was just determined to go all the way. We plan to go out the next day. The tricky bastard requests that I meet him at his apartment. I realize that he intends to fuck me no matter what. I hesitate but finally agree. I mean, I hadn't had any in three months. I was due some. Besides, he is fine.

I am pretty anxious to get my legs around him so I think about him the whole night. He calls me from his job and he is having a conversation with one of his friends. They are speaking Arabic. He asks me a few things and I am amazed at his tenacity because I haven't called him once and it's been three weeks. He asked me about work and I asked him the same. We talked for a while. He wanted to know if I wanted to go to an animal show. I said sure but I wasn't very enthusiastic. For some reason, I was lead to ask him what he wanted from me. This is where I became a little dumbfounded.

"Anwar, what do you want from me?" I have asked this question often enough to other fellas when I needed confirmation of their player status. I had a feeling that this man was not going to give me the typical response but I was ready for him.

"I want a relationship."

"Really?" No you don't, I thought. "You don't appear to be the type who wants a relationship."

"I dated someone for a year before I moved here."

"What happened to her?"

"She still writes but I am too far and we are no longer together." I couldn't believe that the longest relationship he ever had was a year. He even told me that his parents sent him wives but he didn't like them.

"Well, I don't want a relationship right now. I don't have time for one." Maybe I was projecting what I believed was true with him. I had been telling my girlfriends that I wanted a relationship but I certainly didn't act like it. I even said that the next person I dated seriously, would be my husband. Well, I was getting what I asked for right? I think he was good at saying the right thing. What made Anwar different was that he sounds convincing. Other men didn't. Besides, could I seriously date an Arab and then marry him? No.

"Oh," he said. "You are right. I am busy too. It wouldn't be a good time to have a relationship."

Another thing I did that I want to believe was unintentional but I didn't know until later. I would talk to him as if he didn't grasp the English language too well. I wouldn't speak my normal language thinking he wouldn't understand me. He picked up on that because he would say slang to me. I was amazed. I even would think he didn't pronounce things correctly but he did. I was projecting again. Later, I found that Anwar was highly intelligent. Phooey on me. I can be such an idiot sometimes. Anyway, he agreed to my request of being separate but equal.

I anticipated my date not because he was saying the right thing but because he was reaching. He would continue to seek me and I liked the attention. I didn't have to call him but I knew I would eventually because I wanted him to think I was interested too.

When I arrived to his apartment, he was naked. He was just coming out of the shower.

"I am hungry." I say because I can see him refusing me food once he was sexually filled.

"Okay. I will put my clothes on. Come here first." He reached for me and took his towel off. I melted with his touch. His hands were in my suit jacket. He was unbuttoning me. He was kissing my breasts. I ran my fingers through his hair.

"I am hungry," I moan. He is taking off my skirt and stockings.

"I don't eat. I don't like that." I didn't care if he never ate my pussy. I wanted to feel his penis. I am not much into oral sex anyway. It was a waste of a good tongue. I let him feel my juices on his body. I rubbed my pussy on his legs and his stomach. I teased him and he was watching me. He flipped me over and inserted his penis in slowly. I moaned and he slipped his tongue in my mouth. I was panting. Anwar has a delicate touch. He was sensual like myself. I think that is why we continued for so long. It felt good. My focus was getting narrow. I did not like that. What was happening Player One? Nothing, if I could help it.

I was putting on my clothes and he was talking about something on television. "I am hungry." I repeat because there is no way I'm leaving without him feeding me. I stare at him.

"Okay." He starts to put on his clothes. "Where do you want to go?"

"I don't care." I sit on the bed waiting patiently. I think, he knows the routine. Sex isn't free. The charming bastard. I think he is a little scared of me too. I am not talkative and I am watching him.

He took me to lunch and was quiet. I noticed that he tried to walk in the restaurant before me. I wouldn't allow that so we walked in together barely making it. I was miffed and so was he. We ordered and ate in silence. We spoke maybe two words. He was trying to read my mind. When all was done, he walked me to my car (we took separate cars) and he kissed me goodbye in the open. I was perturbed but realized that he was a New Yorker. I had forgotten how New Yorkers behave in public.

I went back to work very disturbed. I liked him. The sex was different. He was different. I made him happy and that was evident. He had funny ways but he was interested in me. Oh well. It was all for naught because I couldn't even consider getting serious with him. I'm sure in his heart he knows this is all about sex. I don't even want to think or feel anything else. Arabs treat their women horribly. I heard all the horror stories. A friend of a friend married one. He beat her and she divorced him. He was a very good looking man too. The woman now looks terrible. I wasn't going out like that. Maybe he would be like most black men and stop calling. He didn't.

I started to dodge him after the fourth heated sex session. I would come over and he would be naked. He would ravish my body. He had mirrors all around the room. He would lay on the floor in front of the mirror or stand me up in front of the mirror. Sometimes, Anwar would entice me to shower with him. I could feel myself losing control.

Not only was I enjoying the sex, I was enjoying the focused attention, the company, and the way his expensive suits were lined up color coordinated in his closet. I had an orgasm just looking in there. He had the best designer shoes a man could have. That turned me on. I get lightheaded just thinking about it. I went there a few times, and when he left the room, I would stare in his closet. This was getting weird. Needless to say, I harnessed my feelings. I started going back clubbing. He called me a few times and I would return his calls. He invited me over and I declined.

At the time, I believed that if I could find someone who could take my mind off of Anwar, I would be able to escape the weird feelings I was starting to have. I began looking for a black man. Someone who would keep me busy. I wasn't having any luck. Maybe I looked desperate. There was a guy at TTR that was interested in me. I entertained the thought but after a few telephone conversations, I wasn't interested. I sat at my desk trying to sort out what was going on. Anwar would call and I would see his number on the phone and not answer. He seemed too eager. He couldn't possibly want me like badly.

Not only was I thinking about what was going on with Anwar, I also had to deal with issues on the job. My pager was going off every minute. Some employees would call 3am or 6am to say they wouldn't be able to come in to work. I had more responsibilities because my co workers won't step up to their share of the responsibilities. I was smoking and drinking more. I wasn't eating. Gina and I would go out almost every night.

"Danny, you look like hell."

"What do you mean?" I really had no idea except I wasn't getting any sleep and was taking valium every night.

"Your eyes are sunken in. I never thought I'd say this but you are too skinny. And you haven't stopped smoking those stinking cigars since I've been in this car. What is going on?"

I really couldn't say. I just didn't have enough time for myself. I was concerned about not being able to get sleep and set an appointment with my doctor for a physical. "Nothing. Just working hard and partying hard."

"You need to quit something. For real."

Anwar invited me over a number of times. I can't remember how he ended up coming to my house but he made it there after I avoided him for a few weeks. I showed him how I liked my sex. He was very quiet laying beside me in the dark. I was feeling a sense of accomplishment. I made the man woozy. What scared me sho nuff was when we were standing in the bathroom and he grabbed my hand and said, "I can see us walking in the mall holding hands." I couldn't envisage anything of the sort. I hadn't allowed myself to think like that. I think the reflection he saw in my eyes when he looked in the mirror disappointed him. I couldn't look at him. I wasn't sure if I wanted to go there with him. No, I knew that I didn't want to go there with him. What was going on here? He even mentioned buying a convenience store near my house. I wouldn't allow myself to think of the possibilities. I would stick to my first impression. Anwar was a man who loved women and who could have any woman he wanted. He honestly wouldn't be able to marry me or anything. He was trying to trick me. Besides, he bored easily. What were his intentions? Did he want me to fall hopelessly in love only so he could treat me like a piece of manure? I just fled a bad relationship two years ago and I barely made it out of there with my sanity. I wouldn't be able to handle another fiasco like that. I reassured myself that I was doing the right thing.

After a while, the dinner and lunch dates dwindled down to 'come to my house' or 'I'll come to your house.' We slipped into the sex fairly easily. I can honestly say that it was good every time. He would call often but I wouldn't call back. I felt that I would easily get addicted. When we talked a little, I found out some very interesting things about him. I was starting to like him even more. I started dating other people. I felt that it was in my best interest to diversify. I met two men at a wedding and there was another dude that I saw on occasion.

Anwar called one night and I returned his call to tell him that I would be going to the club that he frequents because one of my friends goes there. He answered the phone but pretended to be someone else. He said that he wasn't home. Fine. I was puzzled because why would he lie about who he was? Did I seem like I was the type to try to monopolize his time? Or did he want to inflict the same pain in me that I had been inflicting in him? It was beyond my scope of intelligence to believe that this man felt anything from my rejection. After I hung up the phone, I laughed to myself. It would have been to his advantage to have been himself so that I could warn him about my going to the club that he frequents. I didn't want him to think that I was trying to be with him. I wanted to warn him.

I get to the club with my friends from work and he arrives right after us. What a coincidence. He spots me and stays in the car. I see right then that I will have to ignore him. It was okay because I really was looking for fresh meat. It was a bad night because there wasn't any fresh meat to be found. I didn't see Anwar but I wasn't looking for him either. My friends wanted to go to a different dance floor in the club. When we get down there, there he is with his back turned at the bar. I sit down with my friends but I know he knows I am there. He never turns around. I want to go back to the opposite end of the club. I don't want to react the way he thinks I will so I continue to ignore him. No scenes from me. He is with a woman and his friend Alel. I go upstairs and I have a cigar. I sit with my friends and Anwar appears. He starts dancing with some wild woman right in front of me. Kathy notices and says, "Is that Anwar?"

"Yep." Her mouth drops. He gets off the dance floor and puts his drink on the table in front of me. I stare straight ahead.

"Can you believe that?" Kathy wants to slap the shit out of him. She is a feisty white girl. I really like her. We are very much alike.

"No, big deal." I carry on without blinking. I smoke my cigar and watch the white folks dance. We eventually leave and I don't say a word. I am speechless. Maybe I asked for this. No. I don't think I did. He could have said hello. Okay, so I don't call often and I skipped out on a few dates. He wasn't the perfect mate either. I invited him over for his birthday and he never showed up. He didn't even call. That was the beginning of my urge to stay far from him. After being ignored, I couldn't continue with this. The war begins.

Before Anwar, I challenged men. I let them know that I knew every game and I had something for them. It wasn't until Anwar appeared that I questioned my motives. I waited a month to tell him that he didn't have to pretend that he didn't see me at the club. I wasn't going to try to monopolize his time. He lied and said that he didn't see me. I didn't say a word. Then, he told me that a woman ignored him once when he was in the club. So, he knew the game. I said nothing. Of course, I wouldn't show him how devastated I was. As a matter of fact, revenge was sweet. We lay in the bed and I didn't say anything else about it. I shut off any hope that very moment that he had ever been sincere.

Anwar knew that I was really putting a wall up but what impressed me was his tenacity to pursue me. Some days I would agree that he could come over but not be home when he arrived. He took that 45 minute drive and had to high tail it back home. He would call and I wouldn't answer the phone for days. When I did answer his calls, I was nice but not apologetic. He deserved my venom. Sometimes, he would sound rejected and other times he would sound understanding. I didn't give a damn because he was the dummy.

There came a time when I knew I couldn't go on. It was time for me to settle down. I was seeing David Hert and I started seeing him extensively. He was a nice man but not my usual type. I liked him because he reminded me of a high school sweetheart. Anwar called during that time period but I avoided him for four months. He wanted to spend Christmas with me. Things weren't working with David but I would rather sit home and mope on Christmas than to be with someone who didn't respect me enough to speak to me at a club. Anwar called Christmas day and asked me if I wanted to come over for dinner. I declined. I went to visit my grandmother. I was trying to get over David who turned out to be a player. That relationship was a draw. I played him and he played me. I wasn't getting carried away at first and I treated him like I treat everyone else. What betrayed me was my imagination. I wanted to escape Anwar and started leaning to David to help me forget. He started out like most men. Interested and available. After two months, he was gone. Then I slept with his best friend and David was catapulted back into my arms. Finally, he lost interest. It was for the best. I was getting tired of it all and my job was helping to wear me down. I went to see my doctor who advised me that I needed a two month leave of absence, or I would have to quit smoking and quit my job. The stress I was suffering from would send me to a mental institute for sure. I swallowed hard. My hair was falling out and I was emaciated.

"Okay, Dr. Jenssen. What do you suggest?"

"I think you should go to Holly Hill for treatment for two months."

"I don't want to take two months off from work." I was not going for that. I needed to work.

"Okay, I will arrange for you to see the counselor from three to five every evening for two months. You need to work on how to handle stress. You are not doing a very good job of it. If you don't go, your condition will get severe." It felt severe already.

I took two months vacation from my problems. I continued to work until 2pm. I would then head over to the clinic. It is funny how everyone actually looks crazy. I felt very sane. I had a few good sessions with the counselor until she brought up my relationship with my father. I didn't like her anymore after that.

"Why do have such a strong hatred towards men?"

I was being funny when I said, "Because they are the reason for every problem that exists in the world today." I actually believed that.

"Why is that?"

"They can do whatever they want and not have a trace of responsibility for their actions. I don't believe that is fair and I intend to make every one that comes in contact with me pay." I couldn't believe that I had said that. It came out so smoothly. I must have been thinking that all of my life.

"How do you intend to do that?"

"I can be very charming. I especially like men who prey on women. They never see me coming. I treat them the way they've treated women all of their lives and discard them like black oily banana peels."

She cringed at that. "How do you feel afterwards?"

"Good. I never think about them again after I find out they love me."

"Never?" She is staring at me.

"Never." She is writing like a maniac on her little pad. Our time is up.

I debated whether or not I wanted to continue seeing this therapist/counselor/psychiatrist. I didn't see how this had anything to do with my stress and I certainly didn't go there for that. I was going because my doctor said so and I could spend a few hours away from work. I did feel good getting my thoughts off my chest but I didn't want her to hold them against me. I get very defensive when criticized. I guess I should mention that she offered to prescribe something for me but I didn't feel it was necessary if it wasn't going to give me the extra time I needed to eat. I hadn't lost my appetite. I think she thought I was trying to kill myself by wasting away. I didn't believe that. I truly didn't have the time to eat and I was always the type who ate out of habit and not hunger. I would woof down chips and soda and grab a burger in the car but I didn't recognize that as eating and I'm sure she wouldn't either. I pacified her by saying, "I take my vitamins on a regular basis."

"Well, that's a start," she replied. I never cared for other people's opinions and I really didn't think counseling would help. I knew what my problems were. If this woman didn't have a viable solution then this was all a waste. I needed a solution. Something better than throwing myself into my work so much that it takes my life.

Ms. Lanhorn was raising her eyebrows so much that I thought I would walk in there one day and she would have me fitted for a straight jacket. It was like twenty questions and then she'd send me to a group session which I really didn't appreciate. I had no need for others outside of my circle but I am a team player. I just believed that everyone else had a problem and I was there to relieve them or assist in anyway that I could. I did leave the group session with the feeling in the back of my mind that I was flunking.

I mean, I am thirty-one and I have learned to like myself. I am a loner by nature and eclectic. I am at a stage in my life where I don't care if others dig my style or like my mood swings. I couldn't figure out what the source of my stress was coming from. I believed that it was work. After seeing this counselor, I was beginning to believe that maybe there was more to it. I started going to church on a regular basis. I forgot about men and clubbing. Even Gina was having a hard time relating to me. Everything non-Christians did irritated me. This was separating me more and my new found religion brought new looks from Ms. Lanhorn.

"How do you feel?"

"Great."

"How do you feel about men?"

"I feel nothing."

"What do you mean?"

"I have removed my hatred for men from my life and replaced it with my love for God."

"What does that mean?"

"It means that I rely on God to make me happy and not my desire to defeat a man."

She scribbled and scribbled. She may think I am a fanatic, I still didn't care. My two months were up. I could continue but I chose not to. I was going to throw myself into my church. I had quit smoking and drinking along with hanging out with my old set of friends. I got rid of all the phone numbers of men I could care less about and wiped my slate clean. I began to pray and fast from things I loved from things that didn't matter to God.

In January, Anwar called. I had to rid myself of him. I was not the same woman that I was before. I tried to explain that to him.

"Look, Anwar. I am not going to have sex anymore. I am saving myself for marriage."

"What?" Mind you I hadn't had sex with him for eight months because I had been caught up in the David affair.

"I want a relationship and I am willing to wait until I get married to have sex."

"Are you serious? That is good that you want to do that but you like sex as much as I do." I wasn't surprised at his comment. I enjoyed sex with him as much as he did, true. I didn't enjoy it with just anyone but I didn't bother to correct him.

"Well, call me if you want to talk but I am abstaining. Good bye." He was shocked.

"Wait. Are you sure?"

"Yes. Good bye, Anwar."

"Good bye." He wanted to continue to reap sexual benefits from me without having to commit to me. I was done and the thrill of hooking him only to ditch him was gone. There was nothing for me to hang on too. I hadn't spent time to get to know him and it was too late now because I knew I was attracted to him.

I spent four painful months getting to know myself. I didn't like who I was. I found God in the meantime and prayed that he would send my husband. I did a forty day fast regularly. In April, I felt that my husband was coming but as I lay waiting the phone rang. It was only Anwar. He wanted to see me. I was hesitant. It had been four months since I told him I was born again and I was getting good at being celibate. In the past, every time I laid eyes on Anwar we would have sex. There was something magnetic about him. I knew seeing him would be my test. He convinced me to allow him to come over by saying he had a present for me. I bit. I thought I was strong enough. When he came over I didn't see any present. I sat across from him and looked at him sideways. He looked very good but skinny. We both had lost weight.

"Please sit next to me." He pats the couch.

I sat down. He got close to me. He kissed me. He held my face in his hands. He was looking into my eyes.

"Where is my present?"

"It's in the car."

"Well, go get it." This would be the first time he gave me anything. I couldn't imagine. It was Easter and people didn't give gifts on Easter.

He came back with a box. It looked damaged. I looked inside. It was expensive perfume but I couldn't believe that it was for me. It looked used.

"This wasn't for me."

"Yes, it is. Here smell it." He sprayed me. It smelled good but I felt cheated. I couldn't even count this as a good faith gesture. He was addicted to my sex. Maybe, just maybe, he bought that for me for Christmas. He even reminded me that we met in April. I just stared at him. What was he doing? I couldn't think of anything to say. He was right. We first met in April, a week after my birthday but so what. We didn't have any wonderful times to remember. A few dates at a few restaurants and lots of unbridled sex. Mr. Smooth talker got me. He picked me up and even though he wasn't as muscular as when we first met, he lifted me like a pillow. He lay me on the couch and groaned when he touched me. He had that familiar trance like stare. I looked at him.

"I missed you Danny." I missed him too. I dreaded his leaving but I knew he would. He stayed that night but eventually he would have to go. If the

Lord sent him, I believed he would say something to me. He never did. I did notice that before he went to sleep he had his hands together as if he was praying. Why would a Muslim do that? I thought the gesture was strange but I refused to bring up the fact that I wanted a relationship. Didn't he understand the ramifications of all this?

He called two days later.

"Anwar, you know, I wasn't supposed to have sex with you. I have been born again."

"I don't mind." Was his response.

"Well, that means you are my husband in the eyes of the Lord." He had no comment. He wanted to know if he could come see me. I had Bible Study. I also had to pray that the Lord would remove this devil man from my life. He removed the others and I know he can remove Anwar.

Two days later, I called Anwar. "I want you to be my lover." I had talked myself into having another affair with him. If he wanted me and I wanted him, what was wrong with it?

"But you didn't want that two days ago. You wanted a relationship. What happened to the guy you were seeing in January?" I didn't comment on that. He sounded loud too. Excited even.

"I am not ready for a relationship. I thought I was but I'm not." What man wouldn't want his cake and be able to eat it too? I knew this was wrong but I wanted him. Maybe the Lord wanted me to have him. I would say anything to talk myself into being with him. I wasn't going to forsake God and going to church for him. I was not going to start drinking and smoking. Those were things that I would not do again.

My biggest challenge was to stop fornicating. I had stopped for a time period but could I stop enough to wait for marriage? What if marriage was not in my future?

My relationship with Anwar didn't get anymore consistent. He was the only person I was seeing. We went on for maybe three months. Off and on. I continued to pray and fast but the Lord wouldn't remove him. I decided to deny Anwar my body but that didn't work; he just took it as if it belonged to him. I started feeling guilty. I decided to stop speaking to him because it was evident that he only wanted sex and not to make an honest woman of me. I changed my phone number and walked around like a zombie for three months. One day I decided to go to the mall to get some fresh air.

"Danielle. Danielle Mason." What male was calling me by my full name? Should I dare turn around?

I did. It was Anwar.

"Hello, Mr. Sadat. How have you been?" I smiled but I was being very stiff and conservative.

"What happened to you? Why did you change your number? Are you married?"

"No, sweetie. I can't continue to see you if you don't want a relationship. The temptation is too much for me."

He looked very sad. "Can I have your phone number?"

"No. You don't love me. You love sex. I really don't want to talk about this."

"But I do love you. Look at me. I am not doing well. I don't want to be without you." He had stubble on his face and he was upset. "I want to marry you. I don't want anyone else to have you."

"Are you sure?" I was standing in the mall in amazement. This was sheer bullshit. He wanted my pussy. He never had anything like it before. I must admit, the sex was very good. I wanted to believe him but I knew I had to ignore the bullshit. For one, he stopped taking me out long ago. Two, he only called when he wanted sex. And three, if he really missed me and loved me he would have come to see me without calling first. Four, I was born again. I couldn't have sex with him until he married me but if I agreed to be with him that meant we would also have sex. Yet, I was intrigued. I wanted to test the bullshit out—see if it smelled. I should have known better. I handed the fool my digits the whole time reprimanding myself. I know better. I was doing fine without him. I did miss him. I missed his penis.

He called right away. I was flabbergasted. He was trying to put the whammy on me again. He wanted to suck me in. I knew what he was doing. He wanted to hurt me the way I hurt him. But I truly didn't believe that I hurt him. I had just bruised his ego and I was a challenge. This would be the last challenge. Religion or no religion I had to get rid of him for good. I mean, I can't marry an Arab what kind of fool would I be? The word is that Arab men use American women because we are easy targets. I was no target. I was not a sex object. Yet, Anwar wasn't going to stop until I made him realize how unrealistic he was being. This should be easy. Yet, I felt that it may doom me for the rest of my life. I was going against my new found religious beliefs and I was about to plunge head first into uninhibited sex. In a way, I was doing this for me and not Anwar. I needed to get him out of my system as much as he thought he needed me in his. The best way to accomplish this was to spend as much time with each other so that it would become apparent to him that a relationship would never work. Two weeks, tops. Against my better judgment, I asked him to be my lover again. This time he sounded pleased and shocked.

"Why have you changed your mind?"

"I just have." I did not want to get into it. Why did he need an explanation? All he had to do was jump on the gravy train and get fed. When his tummy got full, I expected - no, I wanted him to hit the road and never look back. I was going to make it easy for him this time. To my amazement, it did not happen the way I had planned.

This time when Anwar invited himself over, I agreed. He took me right away. I asked him to leave and he declined. He was too tired to leave. My mouth hit the floor. I think to myself, maybe he doesn't understand "booty call." I didn't complain but now I am suspicious. He was making himself comfortable and making me uncomfortable. I didn't want a relationship and I didn't want to be his ho. I just wanted to be around him. What was I thinking? I had to shake that feeling off. I was not ready for anything serious and especially with an Arab. I'll date any nationality and I'll fuck any nationality but I will not marry any nationality. I will not deprive myself of the unity between a man and woman of the same color, of the same struggle. I could only marry a black man but only when I am good and ready. Did I mention that I was uncomfortable in my own home? He starts telling me what a relationship with him would be like. It is like being married he says because he spends every day with the person. I cringe. I am not ready for whatever he is talking about. I have no response for him. I think he is disappointed.

He sleeps and he doesn't appear to want to leave in the morning. I am undaunted with his showmanship. He is acting. He is a white woman's man. He is primed for them. He wants to know too much about my blackness, my culture and he is too ready to put white people down. I am not impressed or amused. How would he know so much about white people unless he spent time around them? I am not easily fooled. I'd rather not play along. I wonder to myself how long he thinks this will go on. I wonder when I will snap. I snapped on a brother once. He came over and disrespected me in my own home. He came to my house drunk and high. Then he had nerve to get his freak on without considering me. I kicked that motherfucker out on his ass. I pushed him out the front door and put my foot on his ass to speed up the process. I don't have time for ignorance. Anwar was smooth but not that smooth. We slept in two separate corners of the bed. Why was I subjecting myself to this? I deserved something better. Or maybe I shouldn't be having any sort of relationship. Why was I attracted to this man? For some reason, I couldn't get enough.

In the morning, I awoke and saw him staring at me. There was a silence between us. Maybe he was stronger than I thought. Maybe I would be the one to crack. And maybe this was all a game. I had played so many games that it was beginning to get hard to distinguish between the real and the unreal. Anyway, my grandma didn't raise no fool! This started out wrong and there is no turning back. I got out of the bed. He kept laying there. He just didn't get it.

"Listen, sweetie, I am going to work. Lock up when you leave okay." I kissed him on the forehead.

"Danielle, we need to have a serious talk. I need to know where this is going. I can't keep being your sex slave."

What? He was using reverse psychology. I wasn't making him a slave. He was the one who was too busy to be bothered and he never made himself clear. Well I wasn't going to play. I figured I should be honest like only a black woman can.

"I like you Anwar and for a minute you had me thinking I was in love. I know that I am not. I can not marry you. We are too different. You wouldn't be happy with me and I wouldn't be happy with you. I told you that I have changed but I guess my actions speak louder than my words. Today my words and actions are in agreement. I don't want to see you anymore."

Anwar got up and started to put his clothes on. He didn't look disturbed or upset or anything. "You know, Danielle, you never gave me a fair chance and you never treated me very well. I did not do anything to deserve that kind of treatment. If you would just stop searching for something and open your eyes you will see. You will see that everything you think you need is right here. I am not a very religious man and I am not very straightforward about what I want. All I know is that this will never be over. There is something between us. I feel it and so do you. If you never admit it, things will always be this way for you. We will continue to bump haphazardly into each other because we are like magnets." He was fully dressed and looking at me.

"I am getting married." I said it because I wanted him to know that this can end. It can be over. One of us just has to be strong enough to end it. If not him, then me.

His eyes revealed what he was feeling but he never let the look seep into the rest of his body. He remained the same in movement and actions.

"Ok. I wish you well." He was watching me and I was watching him. For some reason we were very angry. He approached me and grabbed me. "Why are you doing this? Why do you hate me? What have I ever done to you?"

"You think you can possess me. You want to make me fall in love so you can mistreat me. The minute I try to get close, you move away. I will not allow you to do that to me. Besides, you have other women. Why not chase them? Once I give in, I am ruined. This has always been a game for you and I know it because it has always been a game for me. Well, I am sorry. Even if this isn't a game, I can not fall in love with you or anyone. I don't want to."

"You pathetic woman. Who did this to you? Someone has made you heartless. The one thing you need more than anything is the one thing you refuse to take. You made me afraid to trust YOU. You are the one who moves away the minute I try to get close. Don't try to project what you are doing on to me. First, you don't want a relationship. Then, you do.

Then, you don't. What do I have to do? I will not beg anymore because that does not work. Must I get violent? Must I? Must I?" He was shaking me.

"Let go of me. Let go of me!" I slapped him. He pushed me on the bed and jumped on me and pinned me down. He slapped me. I tried to get up but I couldn't. "Do you feel better? Is this what you want? You want to hurt me well, you have. Hit me again." He slapped me again. "I will never be with you. You are an animal! Get off of me." I tried to struggle. He had me pinned down.

"I will never let you go. Never. I need you and you need me. You have me confused with someone you used to know. Other men have done things to you but I am not one of them. Now if you don't calm down and listen to me, I will hit you again."

I couldn't believe this. This man was beating me. When he let's me go I am going to hit him with the bat that I had under the bed and I was going to crack his skull. I stopped wiggling. He looked at me but he wouldn't get up.

"I had to hit you Danielle. I had to. Why won't you listen to me? Can't you see that I love you? Why do you push my buttons? Why do you make me so crazy? I really want to marry you. What woman will take me now? You have got me in your pathetic spell and I am hopeless." He lays his body on me. "If I was going to use you and mistreat you, why would I want to marry you? Why would I keep contacting you?" He kissed me all over my face and it felt good. "I'll never hit you again Danielle. Never. Okay? Will you marry me?"

I started to cry because it sounds so real but I was afraid. I allowed myself to trust before and I was deceived. Could this Arab man be real? Did he mean what he was saying? Could he love me? He eased up on me.

"Danielle when we marry things will be different but you will have to change. You have to trust me. Are you willing to change for me? Can you be the woman I need?" He was looking at me and he started to remove my clothes.

"Yes, Anwar." I couldn't believe myself but it felt right. I was feeling differently. I was feeling free.

"You will take care of me and I will take care of you. Can you be faithful to me Danielle?"

He was caressing my breasts and kissing my lips. "Yes, Anwar." This man was bananas but he was what I needed. I needed to stop destroying myself. It was time to stop running and to be conquered. I didn't need a counselor, I needed Anwar.

M. C. Williams

LOVE'S
QUALIFICATIONS

It is cold this May and everyone is hustling and bustling about. Although the springs in Connecticut are never really warm, the weather is the last thing on the minds of young lovers. No matter what the weather does most people are feeling a stirring in their souls that makes them restless. The single are searching for someone to spend their long evenings with, while couples are preparing for their weekends on Mondays. Not everyone is successful in their search for love or in their handling of the relationship after they get it.

This spring most singles and couples spend their nights in the local bars instead of walking in the parks or supping on the veranda in a restaurant. It certainly is not a good time to be alone. The soul gets restless when it has a long winter. Men are conversing with more single women than usual and women are dressing more enticingly. Everyone is looking for that special someone to spend an adventurous weekend. It is out with the old and in with the new and that included relationships. It is on to better things no matter who gets hurt, besides there are other fish in the sea right?

This May and this seasonal mating is different now because relationships do matter and who gets hurt is who gets the last laugh for a lot of people. AIDS is running rampant in every community and it does not discriminate. People are trying to be more conscious by protecting themselves during intercourse physically and psychologically. Psychological protection is very important these days. No one wants to be emotionally scarred. It is all about who withdraws first before they become emotionally involved. Relationships are about meeting certain qualifications rather than pure love. Yet, if pure love were to evolve, how many of us would accept it over our standards? Some of us would rather be alone than to accept love pure and natural without material possessions and preconceived notions. We would rather deceive ourselves than work at making true love satisfying. Others of us avoid the whole process.

Drew notices the weather from his bedroom window and sighs as he gets out of the bed to prepare for work. He goes through the regular routine of washing, fixing coffee, ironing clothes, and cooking breakfast. As he steps out of the door, he notices how unusually cold it is and goes back in to get his trench coat. He sits in his car waiting for it to warm up and thinks about who he is going to call this evening to entertain him. He has plenty of women friends, but he is not serious about any of them. When he first meets a woman, he thinks maybe this is the one. He is always wrong and the relationship turns into the regular routine. He calls them for a fun evening and then drives them home late in the evening. He doesn't think that he is ready for a serious commitment and is not trying very hard to prove himself wrong. Sure, he gets lonely, but he can always find something to do. Variety is good and he has that.

He speaks to the staff as he walks into suite 3D to his office. He begins working on a few projects so that he can go home early. His hopes are dashed when his secretary reminds him of a meeting at one o'clock. He is interrupted again by Claudia, his partner, who needs to speak with him about some accounting mistakes.

"Damn, I won't get home until six tonight."

Drew strolls to her office and waits for her to finish her phone conversation. She is clenching her teeth when he walks in and he notices that she spoke rather sharply.

"Have a seat Drew. I'll be right with you."

She seems to be arguing with her fiance so he busies himself with one of her magazines. Claudia slams the phone down and takes a drink of coffee before she returns Drew's gaze. Argument or no argument, she never looks bothered or upset. He admired her unemotional demeanor when it came to the ups and downs in life. As she speaks, he notices her taking off her engagement ring, but he does not comment about it.

"I swear our accountant drinks before she does our figures!" She says in an exaggerated shrewdness that always makes Drew laugh no matter how serious the problem really is.

"Not Carrie," he adds while smiling.

"Well, I was going to send her a free invitation to an AA meeting, but I guess I'll just have to fire her," she is serious but Drew continues to laugh.

"Is it that bad?" he clears his throat and takes a look at the figures on her desk. "Wow! She is really off. Did we send these already?"

"I'm afraid so. She must be passing the bottle to her assistant because he didn't even catch the mistake. I took one look at it and knew it was wrong. Do I have to do her job too?"

He looks at her face and sees the undisturbed expression that he is so used to. He worries less than he should because she never seems worried. Yet, she always knows when things trouble him.

"Look, do me a favor. On your way out, call the two of them in here and I'll go over it with them. I'll warn her about the mistakes and give her one more chance before we start scouting around for someone else, okay?"

In the office, he thinks about his relationship with Claudia. She is the internal force whereas he is the external. They have been working together for three years and have done rather well together. They are both about the same age; she is six months older than he is. They do not have much of a relationship outside of the office, but are close within its walls. He always found her attractive, but was shot down so quickly upon his first approach that he never tried again. He was to understand that their relationship is purely professional. Besides, she is the type that wants a commitment and he isn't ready for that. He did wonder why she took off her engagement ring. Maybe he should try his luck one more time. If the opportunity is there, why not? Maybe he should give her a little eye contact and see where it goes. Damn, my meeting!

It was late and he is preparing to leave the office when he hears from the other side of the wall that Claudia is typing. He decides to knock on her door. She invites him in and the first thing he notices is that her hair is down. He then notices that her blouse is unbuttoned rather low and her shoes are off. Maybe she does this every evening, but for a man who is trying to get nerve to ask her on a date it makes him uneasy. She notices this and asks if anything is wrong.

"No, I was just wondering if you'd like to get a drink?" He stares into her eyes awaiting her rejection and plans to display a sheepish smile to hide his disappointment. He is surprised when she accepts his offer.

"I just have to finish my last sentence."

They walk to their cars and she suggests that they go to the pub around the corner and that they walk together. He agrees. They talk about his meeting and the accounting figures during their stroll to the pub. He wants to ask her about her ring but decides to wait for the correct moment. They have a few drinks and dance to a few songs. She seems tipsy and he offers to drive her home. She accepts.

"Claudia?"

"Yes, Drew."

"I couldn't help but notice that you took off your engagement ring today. Are you having relationship problems?"

"Well, I'm not engaged anymore, but we still see each other. He still wants to be a part of my life and I don't know why."

"You mean he doesn't care if you have sex with another guy or anything? I wouldn't want to be friends with any of my ex-girlfriends, knowing that they are sleeping with another dude."

"I'm not going to tell him. Now that he is just a friend, that information is off limits to him."

"You're vicious."

"Thank you, but it really isn't his business anymore."

"Do you need me to pick you up tomorrow morning?"

"You have to, I left my car at the office."

"I'll be here at six o'clock sharp."

Finally, after three years he gets a chance to make a move. He has to play his cards right. She is a different breed of woman and he can't let her slip away. He feels exhilarated. He wants to have sex. When he gets home, he calls one of his female friends and he invites her over for a couple of hours.

His mind is on Claudia Amber all night. His heart races when he thinks of her. He wants her more than sleep, but Drew makes himself go to bed. He sees her brown skin when he closes his eyes and feels her lips all over him. He fell asleep with a grin on his face.

The next morning is dreary, but he sees sunshine. He hums in the shower and blasts his stereo while fixing breakfast. Drew eats quickly and goes to pick up Claudia. He wants to be professional because they are going to work, but he notices the difference in his attitude and is sure that everyone else would too.

Claudia is out of her house before he has a chance to turn of the engine.

"Good morning, Drew. How was your night?" Her tone of voice is stern as usual and he loses all his boyish glee that he felt earlier.

"It was quite pleasant. Yours?"

"Just the same, I would say. Do you have a lot of work this afternoon?"

"No, can't say as I do. How about yourself?"

"I'm rather caught up. I should be leaving at two this afternoon."

"I believe that I will be free around that time. Would you like to share dinner with me?"

"Only if we can eat at your place. I don't want to bump into anyone."

"Done."

They walk into the office with the expressions they always have and receive no questioning glances. It is back to work as usual, yet deep in their hearts they know that they are about to tread new ground.

Drew goes into her office at lunch time and she tells him to close the door behind him.

"You know what I always wanted to do?"

"What's that?" His heart is pounding because he thinks she is going to do something freaky. Instead, she gets up and innocently runs her fingers through his hair. She sends chills down his spine. Then, she unlocks the door.

"So, what's for dinner," she asks mischievously. She crunches on a carrot stick.

"Swordfish, baked potato, snow peas, and white wine. For dessert, strawberry sorbet."

"When shall I arrive?" She is still smiling and crunching.

"Is five good?"

"Excellent." He thinks he imagines that she is staring at him and licking her lips. He is so turned on that he wants nothing more than to take her to bed with him. She ends his sexual dreams by discussing new accounts and supply vouchers.

Drew rushes home to begin his meal and to tidy up. He already knows what he is going to say to her to get her in his bed, but he rehearses it again anyway. He does not hid his address book or pictures because that stuff is not important to his final goal. He is a man and of course, he sleeps around. Anyway, that is none of her business. He hopes she isn't going to try to be possessive. What is he thinking? Claudia is just coming over to have dinner, right? She has to know that he is attracted to her. She must know that he wants to sleep with her. Didn't she lick her lips at him? Maybe he was exaggerating, but she did invite herself over for dinner. He begins to think that she definitely wants him too.

She calls at twenty of five to tell him that she is on her way. He has enough time to take a shower and to change his clothes. When she arrives, his heart is in his pants because she looks ravishing. She has on a sexy outfit that he has never seen her wear before. She brings wine and he lets it chill. Everything is perfect. The music compliments the mood and the conversation is very relaxed. Everything about her pleases him. He leads her over to the sofa and brings her a glass of wine.

"You know, I am very glad that we decided to get together. I can not believe that you are sharing wine with me in my home. After three years, here you are. I want you to know that I am very sincere when I tell you that I've always wanted to be with you and that you can trust me. I really want you."

She sips her wine and stares at him with a funny expression on her face. "Really, Mr. Hispera, you don't even know me. I'm just an associate. You just want sex from me."

"It doesn't have to be that way," he says because he doesn't want her to know that he is a dog and he can feel the wheels of fate beginning to turn.

"Oh? How else can it be?"

"I'm not looking for a commitment or anything, but we can see each other."

"We do, sweetie. At work." She is smiling but she isn't being persuaded.

"You know what I mean."

"Do I?"

"Why don't you stay over for a while? Let's start getting to know each other."

"What? Do you know what you are saying? What you are getting into?"

He has a vague idea, but he can't stop himself. He really wants her to stay over. He wants to be around her and maybe it isn't about sex after all. Maybe, deep down he knows he is missing something and he knows that she can supply it. There is something special about her and he wants to experience it first hand.

"It is getting late sweetheart. I have to go." He knows that no matter what he says at this point, he can not influence her to stay. She gets up slowly and he watches her every move. He realizes that he has to try a different tactic.

"I am glad you were able to come over. I'll see you at work." That was it. She is gone. He times her trip home and calls to make sure that she got there safely. The conversation is short and when he hangs up he feels rather low and alone. He can't tell how she feels about him, but he knows that he still wants her. He thinks maybe he should ask her to lunch tomorrow. He looks at the clock and sees that it is early, nine o'clock. Early enough to go out. He calls up a friend of his and they arrange to meet at a local club.

The music is blasting and there are a lot of beautiful women strolling around. His friend notices his mood the minute he spots Drew. He asks Drew who the woman is.

"What woman John?" Drew tries to be smooth and not show his true feelings.

"The one that is on your mind. We are fraternity brothers, you can't hide anything from me."

"Am I that transparent?" Drew throws back a beer and meditates.

"Man, the only time you summon me from the deep is when you want to forget about some unsettling disappointment involving a woman. Always some woman on the verge of captivating your mind. Some woman who isn't easily taken by your charm." John sips his cognac knowingly.

"I fear that this is different."

"Forget it. No woman is worth the trouble. Get the sex and string them along. Never tell a woman how you feel. I know you haven't forgotten any of this, John is looking at Drew suspiciously.

"No, I have not forgotten the ultimate goal of the frat brothers." In the back of his mind, he is thinking of Claudia. His thoughts are innocent. He also realizes how tired he is of the fraternal order of things.

"I saw Karen the other day and she was asking about you. Why don't you give her a call? Hey, isn't that your partner over there?" Drew twists his head in the direction that John is pointing in. He recognizes her sexy shape and hairstyle. It was Claudia alright.

"I could definitely swing with that sister," adds John as he licks his lips and stares in her direction. She walks past them without noticing them. Drew smells her perfume, Volupte. His desire rises to a peak. He gulps down his seven and seven and follows her. She is with a couple of women and she is dressed to kill. She is standing near the dance floor and he stands behind her. She must have sensed his presence because she turns around.

"Well, well. How are you?"

"I'm fine."

"Do you want to dance?"

"Sure." Her body movements are turning him on. They dance close during every song. The chemistry is there. He is getting hard and he notices that she is pressing against him. "Why did you leave me today?" He whispers in her ear only to get a better smell of her perfume.

"You were getting too mushy. If you want sex just ask for it without all the bullshit. You don't have to try to scam me. I've known you for too long."

He could not believe what he was hearing. "Are you drunk? If you are, I am taking you home." Drew steps back to look into her face for traces of inebriation.

"No, I am not drunk. I'm rather depressed and horny." She pulls him closer and rubs up against him.

"So am I. What do you want to do about it?" He grins into her face. His heart is exploding with anticipation.

She leans closer to him and puts her hand in his hair. She pulls his ear to her lips. "Have a condom, will ride. Many condoms, ride long time."

They dance to a few more songs and make plans to meet after the club closes. He wanted to ask her to leave with him right then, but he shakes it off. He doesn't like to appear too anxious. He likes to be in control and never reveal his weakness. He could live off of sex. He didn't need anything else. He goes to the bar and watches Claudia until she is out of sight. He begins daydreaming about what he will do to her once he gets her alone. He will please her beyond her wildest sexual fantasy.

"So, she's the one," states John as he sits next to Drew and stares into his face. "I hope to hell you know what you are doing." Drew ignored his statement. "I've seen Claudia around and she does not play the game the way we'd like her to man." Drew doesn't understand that remark, but he doesn't want to talk to John about Claudia. There are certain things he'd rather frat didn't know anything about.

"Look, can we change the subject?"

"To what? All we ever talk about is women."

"Well, maybe I should leave. I'm not really in the mood for all of this." He leaves John looking after him. Hopefully, he wouldn't realize that it was

Claudia and he would be meeting her at his place. Maybe John would forget about the whole thing.

"Call me, Drew. And for God's sake, don't do it."

Claudia pulls into his driveway seconds after he does. He walks to her car and opens the door for her. He is about to put his arm around her waist, but she stops him.

"Save it honey, you know what I want."

Drew didn't understand why she would say something like that, but he isn't the pushy type. As soon as he shuts the door, she begins to take off his clothes. He carries her to the bedroom. Her lips are all over him. He wants to tell her how much he likes the feeling but she presses his lips closed with her finger. The expression on her face is sad as she says, "You don't have to flatter me with words, just please me." For some reason, he feels as if he has to please her or he'd be ashamed if he did not. He does everything humanly possible to her and is happy to hear her sighs of pleasure and to feel her grab him hard as if to keep herself from dying. He wants to tell her how happy he feels, but he remembers what she said and lays his head on her chest instead. He is only laying there for two seconds when she begins to get dressed.

"Are you leaving?"

"Yep." He looks at her face and realizes that it is the same one she uses in the office. The one without expression. The passion from seconds ago is gone. She is now Claudia Amber, executive and not Claudia Amber, submissive lover.

"I'll see you in the office," she says as she kisses him on the forehead. He doesn't even get out of the bed. He hears the door close quietly and the purr of her engine as she starts the car and pulls off. He honestly doesn't know how to feel about her and has a very disturbing sleep.

That night Drew dreams about his family in Cuba. He longs to be near his family. He wants to go home. He is very lonely in America. He sees his mother's face and he realizes that it is getting older. He hears her say, "Tu familia eres su corazon." He remembers his father who brought him to America when he was thirteen to live with his Aunt Emilia. He tells her, "Mi hijo es muy inteligente. El estudiara aqui." Drew wakes up in a hot sweat. No woman is as important as his family. He says a quick prayer and goes back to sleep.

He doesn't believe that his rendezvous with Claudia is real. He couldn't have slept with Claudia last night. Not Endrique Hispera. He walks to the mirror and looks at himself. He is still young and unmarried. What is he waiting for? The perfect Cuban girl, he told himself. Where is he going to find her, he asks himself. In Cuba, he answers. He would be married by now if he was there. He is determined to go home and bring one back to Connecticut. He looks in the mirror and sees Claudia. Fine brown skin, large brown eyes, sharp nose and high cheekbones. She just isn't Cuban. He blinks his eyes and sees his own large brown eyes, full lips, yellow skin and sharp nose. Not much difference he thinks. Bah! Work and women. Where's the end to it all?

Drew skips breakfast and jets to work. On his way in, Claudia is on her way out. He pulls up next to her car and she rolls down her window. "I'm getting breakfast. Do you want anything?"

"Sure, I'd like an egg and sausage sandwich with waffles and a lot of syrup."

As he walks in the door, the secretary informs him of his daily appointments and makes arrangements with him for future ones.

"Is there something wrong Mr. Hispera?"

"Uh, no, Donna. When Ms. Amber comes back, would you please send her to my office?"

What is he doing? He has nothing to say but a feeling of possession overcame him. He wanted to look at her to see if there was any trace of anything more there. He wants to know how she feels about him, but he isn't even sure about how he feels himself. It would be nice if she would just tell him without him having to ask. Maybe calling her in the office will give her incentive. There is a light tap at the door.

"Come in."

"Did you want me, Endrigue?" She smiles when she says his name and he is amused.

"Yes. Oh, thank you," she places his breakfast on a clear spot in the middle of his desk. "I wanted to know how the receivables and payables were coming along. Not to mention how Carrie is doing with accounting."

"Well to be brief, much better. As far as new accounts, we have very few. The old accounts are paying on time and we are clear of this months bills. I'd also like to say that we have a good profit margin this month. Are you still working on Hartley's company?"

"Yeah, I have another luncheon with him today. Say, would you like to come?"

"Why not? I'm familiar with his file. Maybe I can help you push him into signing a contract with us.

That way we wouldn't need another new account for about two months before our profit margin begins to fall again."

"Great. Meet me here at 1:00 so that we can go over his files before lunch." He watches her as she walks out the door and he gets hard.

The meeting is a success. They finally persuade Hartley to sign a contract with them. It is to go into effect in July. They decide to celebrate over dinner. They meet in a French restaurant in Stamford. She is dressed very elegantly and he is impressed. She has done her hair in a way that he never has seen before. It displays her long neck and her perfectly shaped ears. They talk a great deal and he can not take his eyes off her.

"I bet that you forgot that I am on vacation tomorrow, Mr. Hispera," she smiles and reveals her perfectly white teeth.

"Oh, you are? Are you going anywhere special?"

"Well, a cruise to Cuba and Ochos Rios. It's special to me."

"Really? Any particular reason?"

"No, I've always wanted to go. Aren't you from Cuba?"

"Yes, my family is still there. Would you like to come to my apartment for a night cap since I will not see you for..."

"Two weeks."

"Are you sure you have that much vacation time?"

"Of course," she laughs. "I work very hard, if you haven't noticed. And yes, I will join you for a nightcap."

She follows him home. Before he shuts the door, she presses her body against his. He drops his keys to the floor.

"Claudia..." She puts her tongue in his mouth. He wants to tell her that he can't stop thinking about her. He wants to ask her to stay over. He wants her to know just how much he wants her. Maybe it is better this way. She is a woman of action and she didn't want him to waste words on her especially, if they had no meaning. He has to show her how he feels for her. He begins to kiss her all over. He runs his fingers through her hair. He rubs his cheek against her face. He kisses her eyes and rubs her body gently. After he put the condom on, he enters her slowly and holds her close to him before making love to her. She responds to his every move. When they reach their climax, he notices that she is crying. He can not understand her mood, but he holds her. He wants to ask her what is wrong, but he doesn't know if it is the right moment.

"I can't see you anymore, Endrique."

"Why? What's wrong? Did I hurt you?"

"No, but you will. This relationship has gone beyond the realm of the physical and has reached the emotional. I can't see you anymore because you are wrong for me. I could never marry you, but I could fall in love with you and that could ruin everything. Especially, our business relationship." She starts to put on her clothes and he gets angry. Why can't they have a physical relationship with emotional involvement? They are adults. He watches her and all the while he wants to tell her that he wants more than a physical relationship. He can't make himself say it because he isn't sure if he is saying it because he means it or because he wants instant gratification. A few more nights of steamy sex. He's not going to beg. He's a man. A Cuban man. He is strong and Claudia Amber is not going to defeat him. He hears her leave and remains on his bed staring at the ceiling. She is right. He doesn't need her falling in love with him. He can't promise her anything. Two weeks. What is he going to do in two weeks? He didn't want anyone else. How ridiculous? Since when did he just want Claudia? He can call anyone. Right then, he doesn't want to be with anyone, maybe tomorrow. He decides to call his mother.

"Es Maria Hispera alli? Gracias. Mama, como esta? Si. No. Y papa? Esta frio? Fresco, muy bien. Ay bueno. No esposa aqui. Si mucho de las mujeras son bonitas. Ay mama es muy hermosa." He listens to my mother and longs to go home. He says his goodbyes to the family and looks at the time. Eight o'clock, Friday evening and he is gloating over some woman.

He calls up some of his old college buddies and decides to visit them for the weekend. They go to a couple of fraternity parties, but they are full of young brothers and he feels a little out of place around them. Most of his friends have steady girlfriends and they begin talking about them.

"Hey Drew, are you still looking for the perfect Cubana? You better find yourself a nice black woman like the rest of us and settle down."

"That is fine for you, but I want a woman that reminds me of my mother and my moms is Cuban."

"Man you better hang that shit up. I saw your father and he is the blackest Cuban I ever laid eyes on.

Hell, get a white woman. You look lonely as hell all the time. I don't care who you marry." Kenny takes a drink and Drew knows he is being sincere.

"I'd rather be alone. It's not about color amigo. It's about ethnicity. I want someone that is going to fit in with my family. Someone who cooks what I like to eat and who will like to eat it. It is way deeper than color."

"If that is all it is, I have the remedy for you," says Dave. "Go to a Spanish club. There are plenty all over Hartford. You are bound to find a Cuban in there. I'm getting tired of your ass messing up good sisters anyway. Remember Candy? That sister was hot. Drew just tossed her ass aside."

"Serves her right," adds Jones. "She was color struck anyway. I'm tired of light-skin getting all the fly honeys. But on the real, have you given a sister a chance? You and your crazy friend John have a misconstrued belief about women to start with. I'm waiting for the day you get burned. Then, my friend, no tricks of the trade are going to help you."

"I just want what I want, but I have needs too in the mean time," replies Drew.

"Well, start hitting off some white girls and leave the sisters alone," says Dave.

"How old are you anyway?"

"I'm 34. Why?" Drew knows time is ticking but age is not the issue.

"When do you plan to settle down? When you're sixty? I think your issues are deeper than ethnicity. You have a fear of commitment. Your Cuban ass is screwed up. What was that girl's name from college? Audrey. Her ass messed you all the way up. You better recognize and get some counseling." Jones got up and goes to the bathroom. He was always real about things. Drew liked talking to him, but not on a regular basis. He made Drew feel stupid. There was definitely some truth to the statement.

"No need to rush. You're not missing anything. Some brothers want everybody to suffer with them," says Marc who is 34 and married.

Two weeks comes and goes. It is another Monday morning. Drew makes up his mind that as far as he is concerned nothing happened between he and Claudia. When he gets to work, she is already there. The secretary tells him that Claudia wants to see him. He decides to take his time about it, all the while wondering what she wants. After a few minutes, he decides to go over to her office.

"Good morning."

"Good morning to you and welcome back."

"Have a seat Mr. Hispera. I was wondering if you took a look at these figures." She learns fast. Her attitude was strictly business. Her face was stone. He didn't like it because she was better at it than he was. He was a little unnerved. She hands him the files and he gasps.

"This is incorrect," his mouth is hanging open.

"I leave you here for two weeks and I come back to this nonsense. Must I always check behind everyone's work? What if I wasn't here? What if I took a month off and she sent this figures in? We would be in deep shit." Her whole face is screwed into a frown. He never saw her direct her anger towards him. She was going to make it easy for him to hate her.

"I assure you that this will never happen again." He storms out of her office and has the secretary call Carrie into his office. It was partially his fault for forgetting to check the accounting records right after they were done. When Carrie comes in, he fires her and it was easier than he had imagined considering it was his first time ever doing it. Now, he was left with the task of finding her replacement. He is fully capable of running the office on his own. What did Claudia mean when she said what would happen if she left? He would hire someone to take her place. Of course, it wouldn't be that easy but it could be done. Couldn't it? Damn! Why did he always let his emotions take control of his actions? Why did he involve himself with his business partner? He had a lot to lose. Drew is pacing the floor when he hears a tap on the door. He is at the height of his anger.

"Come in," he bellows. He is surprised to see Claudia.

"Are you okay?" she doesn't look the same as she did in her office. Her edge has dissipated.

"Of course not! Incompetence. I need someone reliable and competent."

"I missed you."

"What?" he is shocked at her forwardness. He wants to tell her he missed her too, but he does not. He never wants to be rejected the way she had rejected him. He refuses to suffer the same humiliation.

"Can I see you tonight?" He sees something in her eyes. She has never been vulnerable in front of him, but he withstands the temptation.

"No, I have plans," it hurts coming from his lips, but he has to punish her and himself. He can't go any further than sex with her and he doesn't want her hanging the sex over his head if things turn sore. He can't jeopardize his business any further. The company may not matter to her, but it matters to him and he'd better start showing it. She was right in rejecting him in the first place.

"Fine, Mr. Hispera. I can keep this on a business level. I'm sorry for intruding, she is an iceberg and he does not understand her. Claudia was one moody woman. She quietly leaves his office. She leaves work early and doesn't say goodbye.

He hates himself during the drive home. He hates himself when he walks into his empty home. He hates himself for even wanting to call John. He dies a million deaths when he does.

"Juanito, que pas…"

"You're hooked and you want to forget. Didn't I tell you it would happen? Why didn't you listen to me?"

"Look, I just called because I want to go out."

"Right. After three weeks, you suddenly want to go out. Your old girlfriends are mad at you. They say you don't return their calls. Anna doesn't want to see you anymore but you know her, she always says that."

"Forget them. I want new chicks. Let's find a Latin Club."

"Endrique, I hate to tell you man, but you have exhausted the supply of women in Hartford. There are no new chicks. You would have to move out of this country to find new women. Anyway, they are all the same after a while. All you have to do is apologize to the old ones and you're back in business."

Jones was right, he and John have problems. He didn't want to apologize. To whom? For what? So, he neglected a few women. "What did I call you for?" he hung up the phone.

Drew decides to watch television, but chances his mind because he hates television. He never enjoys anything besides sports. He sits down for a minute. He thinks about Claudia. Maybe he should apologize to her. She is his business partner and he needs to explain why they should end things. He owes her that much. Her phone rings but no one answers. He decides to go to the gym. The workout does wonders for him. He stays extra long because he wants to make himself exhausted enough to go straight to sleep when he gets home. Drew feels a spurt of energy and decides to stop by Claudia's house. Her car is in the driveway. Maybe she doesn't want company. Maybe she was home when the phone rang. Never mind all that, he knocks on her door.

"Who is it?"

"It's Endrique."

She slowly opens the door and her two dogs were about to spring on him. Thank goodness the screen door was locked.

"Let me take them to the basement." Drew peeks in. It looks nice and cozy. He expects the house to smell like dogs but he is pleasantly surprised. It has a clean odor and looks modern. She has paintings everywhere and they look expensive.

Claudia lets him in and shuts the door. "Have a seat. Would you like some wine?" He nods his head and she heads for the kitchen. She returns and sits across from him in a King Edward arm chair.

"I like your mixture of modern and antique furniture. I feel at home here. I am impressed." She says thank you and keeps her eyes on him. She does not hold up her end of the conversation. She is probably trying to figure out the impetus for the visit.

"Why did you leave me the way you did?" he demanded to know.

"What do you mean? Let's just skip to what's real. You are all wrong for me. You are Cuban and Catholic and I work with you. All the wrong things wrapped up in one."

"We have a lot in common in that respect. I am on a quest for a Cuban woman and I want to be with someone who can relate to me."

"What kind of quest where you on in black clubs sleeping with black women? I never saw you with a Cuban. On a quest for what? It looks like a quest to submerge yourself in meaningless relationships in order to make it through. I gave you what you wanted. You didn't want an attachment. You, Mr. Hispera, were the one who did not want to go any further with me today. You made me realize that I made the right decision in disconnecting myself from you. We are business partners and can never have a relationship. So, why are you here?"

"All I know is that I stopped seeing other women. I think about you constantly. I always imagined that I would marry a Cuban woman because that is what I am and who I am. I never wanted to get serious with anyone. All I wanted was sex but I realized that I couldn't be that way with you. I know too much about you. We've worked together for three years and I like your presence and our friendship. I like everything about you but you were never available to me. It wasn't until you broke off your engagement did I realize that I may have a chance with you. I didn't realize that it was more than sex that I was seeking from you. I came here I guess, because I want to try this relationship thing out. I know I say a lot of things that I don't mean but this time I am speaking from my heart."

He doesn't know what to expect from her long silence. He recognizes that expressionless look on her face. He feels angry because he can feel rejection about to surface. She was just engaged, why would she want to get involved in another relationship? Maybe he is rushing her and he needs to wait.

"You know, Endrique, I went to Cuba with my fiance. I wanted to rebuild what we had lost. I had been with him for ten years and felt that he was worth it. You know what happened to me after I left your house? I realized that all of my ideals had crumbled. Everything that I thought I wanted in a man, I realized that I never had it with my fiance and I may never get it with anyone. What I had was a fairy tale. I never had love from him because I created that relationship. I was working too hard. Not because of love, but because I wanted it to be perfect. You are not perfect but I am willing to sacrifice all of my ideals for you. I am willing to forget who I am and what I am to be a part of you. I wanted to tell you that earlier today." Tears are streaming down her face. She lowers her head because she doesn't want him to see her crying.

He walks over to her and kneels in front of her. He rests his head in her lap. He belongs with her and he realizes how close he was to losing her. No one should ever deny themselves the chance to experience love just because it doesn't come in the package you imagine it in. Love just happens. When two people feel it at the same time they should try to compromise and communicate. There is really nothing more important.

NO LIMIT

He was leaving me again. It was sad to see his back to me. No kiss this time as he walked out the front door. He turned around but I shut the door. I frowned. I went back to my room and lay on the bed. Why Lord? Did I deserve this pain. Time and again. Doesn't he know? I sigh deep. No he doesn't and if he did, so? So. There are probably plenty of women. I am just one of many and not one in particular. He doesn't think of me as he drives away. It will be another day or week or month before…I sigh deep. I close my eyes and I try to remember him. I smell his scent on my sheets. I pull the covers up. I think I have to exist without him and eventually, never more. Today, I feel the pains of love that would never materialize. It was just sex. I need to wake up.

I go directly to the shower. I cry in the water. I feel better when I think of the children. I will throw myself into the children at the orphanage. I think of my little ones, black and brown and tan and peach. So

111

sad. It is early. I'm not hungry so I get dressed and grab my car keys. I feel alone as I take that 60 mile trek through dirt roads and trees. It is so peaceful and the extra 15 minutes are well worth it. I pray while I drive that I get the strength to leave that poisonous man alone. He is stealing my joy, he is removing my focus. I prayed that others would be removed and the Lord was good to me. This man is my test. I am falling horribly. I say, "No sex this time Marisa. Just talk and then send him home." I never can. There is something about him. It is almost as if he can read my mind. He calms me and soothes me. He renders me speechless. I am hypnotized by his body and his eyes. He looks at me and I melt. He kisses my lips and it's all over.

"Oh my God!" I slam on the breaks. It is too late. I hit the deer. He falls back dazed. I stay in the car waiting to see if he is still alive. He is. He gets up and runs off. I get out of the car. My right front fender is destroyed and hanging off. That is what I get. I think to myself. If I hadn't been sinning with the devil this would never have happened. I remove the fender and put it in the truck. The deer took the whole thing clear off. I sit behind the wheel. What next? I call my insurance company. They tell me they can handle everything first thing Monday morning. I feel better. I don't even have to call the police because it was an act of nature and I'm covered. I thank God and start the car. I creep along now because I'm looking out for deer.

I feel an overwhelming happiness as I see the orphanage. I hurry out of the car because I am a little late. I walk in and smell lunch cooking. I visit a few of the children before heading to the cafeteria. When I get to the kitchen, I immediately put on an apron. Hedda rushes in the kitchen with a few trays.

"You're a little late. Are you okay?"

"Yes. Just had a little collision with a deer." I start washing dishes because I am not ready to face the noise in the cafeteria.

"Oh, no. You should stop by a hospital. You may have hurt yourself."

"No, I'm fine." I busy myself with mind less work hoping to avoid Hedda's gaze because she knew too much about my situation and I didn't want to talk.

"Is he gone?" she whispers. I don't answer. I want her to go away. "Good riddance. The devil has…"

"Listen, it's my fault for taking him back. When he comes knocking, I'll be there to open the door. I'm just weak." I took the baked chicken out to the hungry children. The noise turned into silence. The children always stopped talking when the food arrived. Many of them had their little mouths open in anticipation. Tummies growling and legs swinging. I served the chicken and Hedda followed me with the peas. Daniel had the rice and was serving the other side of the room. Julia came out with the punch and the children were all consuming some portion of their meal. I shouldn't have come in because looking at the children didn't make me feel any better. Yet, I came in because they need me more than I need them. Or did they? I was beginning to question everything I did because of Mark. Was I doing things to keep from thinking about him? Is that so awful? Children are benefiting from your lack of love, Marisa. If God says this is how your life should be, if the reason you volunteer your time is to keep your mind from being idle then, so be it. Enjoy what you can, Marisa.

While the children ate, the rest of us went back to the kitchen to clean up. After the kitchen is complete, each one of use gets a group of the kids and takes them on a trip. Many times we go to the park, or the community center, or the museum. The orphanage has six vans donated to us from my church. It took a lot of plate sales and auctions to get the money but it was worth it just to see the smiles on the little faces.

All of the time spent in church and still Marisa couldn't find a respectable mate. Everyone had advised her to find a decent man from church because that was the only place a decent man spent his time. That was an untruth if ever one was told. The men who attended church were sick men. Men who needed guidance. Men who used to and sometimes still did things they knew were not good for them. Now, there isn't anything wrong with a man going to church to seek guidance but it definitely isn't the place to seek a man. Marisa knew that from experience. She dated two men from church to know the reality of that situation. The first man had been married twice. He was nice enough but he liked his liquor. Not only did he like his liquor but he liked his women loose and drunk. Bad situation. The other man was good enough but he liked to go to the clubs on Friday and Saturday nights. After long consideration, Marisa realized that church is for praying, fellowship, and healing. Hunting for a man would only lead you to an animal whether in church or anywhere.

Marisa met Mark in the grocery store. They were buying steaks and when she went to pick up a pack he went for the same one. Their hands touched and she drew hers back quickly. He said, "I'm sorry. If you want it you can have it."

"That's ok, I'll take this one." Marisa reached for the one next to the one in his hand and he put his hand on that one. She knew that he was flirting and she looked into his eyes for the first time. He was smiling. He leaned on the freezer and folded his arms over his chest.

"It looks as if we want the same things. Maybe that's just a coincidence, maybe not." He had a slight accent. Marisa later found out that he was from Portugal. He had beautiful green eyes and muscular hairy arms. He had full lips that he was licking and a crooked grin.

"That depends. I just want a nice cut of steak. It looks to me that you have an appetite for bigger things." I don't know where I found those words and the courage to say them but I liked this new spell that was taking over me.

He laughed as he said, "You are pretty and witty and you like steak. Is there anything else I should know about you?"

"I like flattery." I picked up the original pack of steak and threw it in my cart. I started to roll the cart away when he started to tell me how he cooks his steak. I stopped because it really did sound appetizing. "How long do you marinate it?"

"Thirty minutes. The meat slides right off the bone." The way he looked me over made me feel like that steak. "Maybe you'd like to come over for dinner." He smiled again.

"I don't know. I don't even know your name."

"It's Mark. I'm single and I'm harmless." He was smiling that confident crooked smile.

"Let me tell you a little about myself, Mark. My name is Marisa. I go to church every Sunday and any other day when something is going on. I donate a lot of my time to charity and I'm single." I was smiling but only to return his smile and not for any particular reason.

"Maybe you would like to have some company when you go to church?"

My heart skipped a beat. This man knew what to say to me. That line about church strung me in. "Really? That would be a nice way to get to know each other before you cook me that steak." He had me and he knew it. He whipped out his business card like an old professional. It had the name of his business and all of his numbers on it. Mark Pillard. The beginning of the end for me. He took out another card to write my name and number on. After our meeting, I never felt more alive.

Mark and I had a whirl wind relationship for about three weeks. We went to church and out to eat. He wined me and dined me. I was adamant about breaking my celibacy and I told him that.

"How long have you been celibate, Missy?"

"Four years."

"Don't you think it's time?"

"Maybe." Maybe but I was saving myself for Mr. Right. I wasn't sure if he was that person and I wasn't in any kind of rush.

Day one of week four. "Missy, I think about you all the time. I don't want any one else."

Day two week four. "Missy, I think we should consider making a commitment to each other. I am not seeing anyone else. Are you?"

Day three week four. "Missy, I want you to meet my family."

Day four week four. "Missy, I want to meet your family."

Day five week four. "Missy, I love you." Most women are suckers for those three little words. I am a sucker. He had my clothes off within a minute and the sex lasted about that long. Now, if he had gotten the sex and left maybe then things wouldn't be so hard for me now. But he didn't. He stayed the whole day and part of the next day. We made love for as long as he stayed. He was fast but consistent. When it came time to go to church he had an excuse. He said that he had some business to take care of that Sunday. I didn't question him. The last thing a person needs is a guilt trip.

When the fifth week came around, I didn't see him until Wednesday. He stayed for two days and he made an excuse for the rest of the week saying that he needed to catch up on week. Still no guilt trips from me. As a matter of fact, I had some things I needed to do to keep myself busy. I did feel used. I was doing a good job of abstaining before he came along. I could only blame myself. I knew the game from way back when I was heavy into sin. It was one of the things you don't forget.

I didn't call him much to begin with and I stopped calling all together. I made myself busy for the next few weeks to follow. When he would come to visit, I wouldn't open the door knowing he could very well see my car. He would call and I wouldn't answer the phone. He left six messages a day. He broke me down with his persistence. I couldn't figure out why, after he had gotten what he wanted, would he bother to keep pursuing me? I opened the door to sin when I answered the phone. Something about his voice made me melt. I would give in to his pleads. It just didn't make sense to me. After that rendezvous, I ran to my pastor. I told him to pray for me. I needed the devil removed from my life. My pastor who never appeared to be profound before said something that I will never forget. "Child," he began, "I can pray 'til Armageddon but if you don't know in your heart that what you are doing is wrong, you won't stop." When he first said it, I thought to myself that we had a third rate clergyman as the head of our church. He couldn't help a fly. The more I pondered over it the better I felt about his wisdom. Somewhere in three weeks, I allowed myself to think that being with Mark was ok. I had fallen into something. I won't say love. Maybe I fell into lust or infatuation. I began to lock myself away in my house to contemplate the ways of this evil world. I was now a lost sheep. I didn't want to deny myself his pleasure but I didn't want to fall back into my old evil ways. The devil had me on a limb.

Marisa drove the van to Kelsea Park. It was hot out, but not hot enough to be hazardous to the children. She slid the doors open and the children peeled out. They ran as fast as their little legs would carry them to the slides and the swings. Marisa loved coming to the park because she could take out a novel and read.

Every now and again she would peek over the book to check on the kids. Some times she would have to diffuse an altercation or tend to a minor wound. Her days in the park were the best of her life. Marisa raised her head to check on the children and saw a familiar figure holding two small children. He had one by the hand and the other on his shoulders.

"My God," she whispered under her breath. It was Mark. Did he have a secret life that he didn't bother to tell her about? She kept looking in his direction without averting her gaze. He felt that someone was peering at him and he looked in her direction. There was the smile she was so accustomed to seeing.

"Missy! How are you? Where have you been?" He was so amicable that she couldn't be angry at him for being himself.

"I've been busy with the church, that's all. You know me, dedicated church lady."

"Yes, I know." He was still smiling.

"So, what brings you to the park?"

"My kids. Lisa and Leon." Mark said it without flinching but Marisa was unmistakably unnerved.

"You never mentioned that you had children." Right at that moment, John came over to tell on Kim. She had been throwing dirt on some of the children. I told him to tell her to come to me. He ran off towards the sand box. Marisa turned back to face Mark. "Do you have a wife too?"

"No. I just have my two kids. They live with my mother after their mother died."

"Oh, I'm sorry." I was sorry but I was a little upset about not knowing any of this before.

"I miss you Marisa." He seemed sincere.

119

"I miss you too, Mark."

"Do you really?"

"Yes, but I don't know how far we can go or how far you want to go because every time I think we've made a connection, you leave."

"I'm sorry about that. I don't want to stay away from my children too long. I didn't mention them because some people don't take to children too well."

Kim came over and sat next to me. She knows the routine. Misbehave and you get time out. Mark looked over at his kids and went over to get them. He introduced them to me. They looked about nine and ten.

"So who is this?" His smile was back and the kids ran to the sandbox. Kim was wiggling and squirming by now. Her five minutes were up.

"This is Kim. Say hello then you can go play but no throwing dirt. OK?"

"Ok. Hello Mister." She ran off before he could say anything back.

"Wow, she must really like the sandbox." Mark turned around to see Kim dive in kicking up dirt. Technically, she hadn't done anything wrong. I went over to reprimand her and sat back down. "How many kids do you have with you today?"

"Twelve balls of fun and excitement." I neatly closed the novel after jamming the bookmark in between the pages.

"What are you reading?" He was a cannon of inquisitiveness.

"A Christian book." That wasn't entirely true. It mentioned that the characters went to church but that was all it said about God.

"I read that. It has a great ending. Did you get to the part where Sharon meets her uncle?"

"No, and please don't tell me any more. I like to be surprised." I was surprised already. He read this book? There was a lot I didn't know about Mark.

"I want to see you after I take the kids home."

"Why not come see me tomorrow after you put them to bed? I'll still be around God willing."

"Yes, God willing." He was quiet for a minute as if he had to get something off his chest. "The reason I stopped going to church with you is because I take the kids now. I want to thank you for reminding me about how important it is."

I was touched. There was no better reward. When Mark left me in the park, I didn't feel abandoned. He had two perfect reasons for leaving me and I could live with that.

M. C. Williams

DOMINIQUAE

It was six o'clock in the morning and she was sitting at the table eating breakfast in her Victoria's Secret robe. Her cook prepared an old southern dish of apple fritters, cheese grits, toast, and fried fish. Her hair was in place and she sat in the dining area alone. She is childless and husbandless at the age of thirty-four. This was unimportant to her because she had more important things to take care of her in life. After eating, Dominiquae Russell lit a cigarette and proceeded to stare out of the window. She had five minutes before her bath would be ready and forty minutes before her car would be waiting out front. Every minute of her day was accounted for because she had to keep everyone and every thing in line. Dommie began to frown when she thought of all the things she would have to accomplish. She had too much to do. Mondays were always the worst days because large loans were made over the weekend and old debts were supposed to be paid on Mondays. The office was always a mess and people were always rushing around to take care of business; sometimes, at the expense of other employees.

"Ms. Russell, your bath is ready."

"Thank you Banks."

Dommie walked up the one hundred and six flights of stairs to the sixth floor where her bath was and where her clothing was laid out. She always wore a black suit on Mondays. Jonathan bathed her and dressed her. Helena did her hair and made up her face. On her way to the car, her body guards and associates accompanied her. Max, Marcus, X, and Sheila all followed her from the fifth floor. Donna, Train, Lonnie, Jerome, Cal, and Renee followed her from the fourth floor. Kalil, Malik, Fiodora, Donnell, and Keyba followed from the third floor and Monty, Muhammed, Moses, and David from the second. Remus opened her door and Moses, X, Train, and Keyba followed her in.

Each employee took a glass of Vodka from the table before the limousine pulled off.

"We are short 300 thousand. I called Shorty this morning and she said that money was still coming in but slowly," replied Train.

"Maury said that they had to bust up two people already who were late for their 5 am and 5:30 am drop offs. Between the two there was 26 thousand each," added Moses.

"Three people called in for extensions. Joseph Lieberwitz, James Palmo, and Anthony O'Connell. They have until next Monday at 6 at 30% interest compounded daily. They total 100 thousand," said Keyba.

X waited a few minutes before he added his findings to the report. Everyone took sips of vodka and waited. "I found Marshall Meed in Ireland. Terminated. I found Donny Diangello in Sicily. Terminated. I found Brandon Wilcox in South Africa. Terminated. Their assets bring in a total of 403 thousand. It has all been deposited."

"So what you are saying is that we have only 103 thousand over the top?" Dommie was shouting. They knew she was going to have a fit but that was her typical Monday morning style.

"What the fuck am I going to do with 103 thousand, wipe my ass? Aghhhhhhh! I am going to lose control," she muttered as she proceeded to smash the vodka bottle.

"Keyba, you call those mutha fuckers and tell them that they have until tomorrow with 50% interest or they will be floating in a river. X, I want you to find two more deserters by Thursday and wipe their fucking assets clean. Train call Shorty right now and get the figures. Moses, you tell Maury to bust mutha fuckers who are even two seconds late, you got it? I swear if I don't have 600 thousand by Thursday, one of you bastards are gonna disappear foreva. Remus," she screamed, "get these assholes outa here."

"Yes, boss." Remus slammed the breaks. Everyone started scrambling out as Dommie threw the Vodka bottles and glasses. Train shouted out the figures as he fled the flying glass. "We are down 150 thousand." Dommie threw a bottle right at him. He stepped aside and shook his head.

When they pulled up to the office, her hair was a mess, and so was the limousine. She looked in the mirror, put on her hat, and waited for her guards. "Remus, clean up this mess, she muttered as she walked past him. She was all smiles when she walked into the building and saw how busy everyone was. "Good morning, boss" was heard from every direction. Dommie walked into her office alone. She lit a cigarette and gazed out of the window for a minute. The phone rang.

"Who the fuck is it Maria? I just sat the fuck down. I didn't even get a chance to look at the figures. It better be fucking important."

"It's the FBI," she whispered.

"What the hell do they want?"

"The usual."

"Transfer them."

The line clicked over and I heard Arnie breathing hard.

"No, dammit, so don't even ask me," Dommie said before he opened his mouth.

"Look Dommie, you know I wouldn't ask you if I could avoid it."

"Avoid it. I will never forgive your people for getting S killed. You tell them if shit like that happens again I will blow the fucking building to pieces!"

"I told them the first time you said it Dommie. You know, I only call you when the job is too hard for us. Your people are the best at tracking and terminating. You know we pay big."

"Look, I will loan you two guys but I don't want your people involved at all. Don't you train those bozos to do back up work? If someone even gets a scratch, I'll blow your fat Arnie-ass up. 22 Springfield Avenue, two boys, and a fat ass wife."

"How did you get that information? Dommie, I swear…" I hung up. I called Maria and told her to send S6 and S7 to the Bureau. That would be a few extra million next month if my men didn't get killed. If they did, I would only break even. It takes a million to train my men to track and terminate individuals without leaving a trace. The Bureau was eating up my men two at a time. It was a conspiracy.

I looked down at the stock figures, the z-bonds, and t-bonds. I looked at the real estate figures, the club figures, and retail sales at various department stores that I bought out. The economy wasn't doing well but my figures were high. The phone rang.

"Yes, Maria."

"One of Pinkie's boys wants to see you."

"Really? Send him in." I am so sick of the mafia and their bullshit. I polished my 357 before he knocked on the door. I put it on my lap and continued to look at the stock figures as the stooge walked in. I hated him immediately. I told the Don about sending pasty white Italians to my office.

"What the fuck do you want?"

"The boss…"

"What the fuck did you say?"

"I mean, my boss don't like that you took out one of his boys for 50 thousand."

"So! Is that all you came over for? He must not like you very well, I shouted. I stood up and took out my piece. I cocked it at his head. Whitie was nervous.

"N-n-no," he stammered. "He wants me to tell you to hand his boys over to him next time and he'll settle all debts."

"Next time. Next time?" I shot at his kneecap and blew the shit off. I laughed at his facial expression. "You tell your boss that the next time he sends some pale muthafucker in my office, I'm gonna go right over there and blow his farting Italian ass off, got it?"

I pressed the intercom. "Send someone up here to get this spaghetti boy outta here."

"Sure, Dommie, but did you forget that you have a meeting in thirty minutes with the CIO of trade and commerce? Remus has the location."

Someone came and dragged the white boy out by his suit collar and he was hollering all the way out the door. I made a note to call the don so that I can explain how the fuck he upset me so that he wouldn't do it again. Sometimes, he gets amnesia. I looked at my watch and decided to get going; I liked to be early for meetings. Someone was already in my office mopping up the white boys spaghetti sauce that made a big puddle on the floor and a thick red line down the hall. I saw the screaming pizza on my way out. "Tell the don, I will call him in the very near future." I stepped on his good knee with my nice six inch heel. He called me a bitch. I turned around to shoot him in the head but realized that he was the only one who could relay my message; the don was getting smart. He usually sent three guys and one would return lacking the ability to take in air. "You lucky meatball." I got in my car and drove off.

I never took anyone with me to lunch because it cost too much and looked too suspicious. I am always surprised when no one tries to whack me. I mean I am a defenseless woman. No guards, no nothing. It never happens. I wish someone would try their luck, especially on a Monday or when I am PMSing. Besides, I'm no coward, I can take care of myself. When I got to the restaurant I felt for spaghetti and meatballs basted in white marinara sauce. My company showed up a little after I did. He liked being early too. The waiter came over and looked from me to my guest. He finally decided that I was the big shot and asked me what we would have. I ordered white wine and the Italian dish I had been salivating over. Michael Fuentes had the same. It was customary to eat and talk business with black people and I was pleased that Fuentes knew the rule.

"So, you want to get into the BMW business by trading with Germany. Big bucks for nice beemers. I spoke to JQ and we can work something out. She wants you to buy into the company at 20%, that way if things turn out well, everybody makes a lot of money.

"Right, but if I fuck up, I have a lot more to lose."

"Exactly, but she does not believe that you will fuck up," he grinned and ate a meatball. I noticed how brown his skin was.

"How much is twenty percent worth right now?"

"300 thousand."

"You'll have it this evening at five."

"Great. Your BMW's will be in the mail April 3rd and the invoice will be sent when the check lands on JQ's desk. Remember you take 20% of the profit from whatever you sell and you know the rest depends on the stock market."

"Fine." I noticed that he was looking at me. I returned his gaze.

"I feel for dessert," he announced.

"There is some in my limousine, I didn't wait for him to respond. I called the waiter over and paid the bill. I told Remus to cruise around the Atlanta area. Michael and I drank our drinks quickly and I turned on the CD player. He pulled up my skirt and ate me. He was very good at it. He zipped down his pants and slipped on a ribbed lubricated thin condom. I screamed as he inched his fat dick in slowly. The limousine movement and his slow motions made my orgasm vibrate throughout my body. He rubbed my body and sucked my breasts. After the explosion subsided, we did it doggy style until he came.

We laid around with our clothes half on, I was smoking a cigarette and he had a Havana. I asked him where he was from and he said Puerto Rico. He ate me again.

"Nice place. Where should I tell my driver to drop you off?"

He didn't answer me. I pulled the back of his hair.

"The airport," he said and went back to licking and sucking. When I came, he drank me. I thought about keeping him around for a split second. I hadn't had it like that in a long time. I liked being sexually frustrated, it makes a woman mean. I needed the edge in my line of work. I didn't think Michael was ever going to stop. We pulled up to the airport. I pulled his head up again. "We're here."

"Do you want me to stop?"

What was this, twenty questions? I didn't want him to go but I wasn't the one who had to catch a plane. "Yes. Tell JQ that she did good." I was hoping my girl grew men like that somewhere.

"Do you ever come to Puerto Rico?" Michael was getting dressed and licking his thick brown lips. He was very attractive.

"Yeah." I watched him brush his hair.

"I would really like to see you again. Look me up." He was staring at me. I was still undressed and drinking Merlot. He grabbed my breasts. He kneeled in front of me. "I understand that you are a very powerful woman. I love powerful women. Love them," he curled his tongue around the word love.

I looked at him as he rubbed his face on my breasts. What was he getting at?

"I don't want to stay in Puerto Rico. I need someone like you." I pulled his head back by his hair. I licked his neck and chewed on his fat bottom lip.

"I will think about it." For some reason, I couldn't tell him no fucking way. He picked up his briefcase and left. I went back to the office. The sign in front of my building said, "Mecca Financing: We've got your back." I laughed.

I rushed through the office and noticed the new loans that were issued. I wrote all of the names in the new loan ledger and wrote all of the figures down in another ledger. I had ten minutes before closing time. I peeked out of the window and saw the limousines waiting and a few of the guards congregating outside. I went to my car and we took off. I walked straight up to my bath and soaked for a few minutes. I went to dinner in my robe and was accompanied by all 64 members of the house. Most of the people were in my immediate family while the others were the family of business associates. We never talked business at the dinner table. The last time someone even mentioned money, I flew into a rage. Food went flying and every one got quiet. Some of the children started crying. No one has talked business at the table ever since. My family is curious about my career but no one asks questions. They wonder why I get so many phone calls and why it is necessary for so many of my employees to live with me.

After dinner, I took a dip in the pool. Maxine came to me with the phone in her hand and told me that Frederique was on the line.

"Tell him to come right over."

"Yes, Ms. Russell."

My investment banker Frederique has it bad for me. He is close to being fired. He was coming over more than necessary and he was becoming annoying. He wasn't even my type. I would give him the benefit of the doubt, maybe he would actually have a work related issue. If not, he was going to be dismissed. I was not interested in overly eager individuals who wanted a steady relationship with a powerful woman. He would say anything but the truth. He was trying to be deceptive when he was transparent. I had enough of phony-baloney. The only person who lit a spark was Michael from this morning. Even that was unusual. JQ was always sending men but not one until today made Dommie feel like a woman. What was it about that guy? His bluntness got her. He loved power and she could dig that. She loved it too, obviously. With the good comes the bad and he has to be made aware of the bad of the situation. He even told her to look him up. Michael liked to play cat and mouse and she was the pussy to play.

Michael went to the bathroom at the airport to rinse his mouth and to straighten himself up. He loved working for his sister. JQ got more business from him than any of her other sales men. He had been begging for the Russell account for years. She wouldn't let him near it. It was too dangerous. The other sales men didn't have a personal connection to JQ so they were expendable. Besides, Dommie was crazy. She would do whatever her head told her to yet, she had the money to back her up. Dommie owned everything in Atlanta. JQ definitely wanted a piece of that action. The only reason Michael received this one opportunity was because the regular sales man had another assignment and Dommie had a small complaint, the guy was fugly—fucking ugly. It almost cost JQ 300 thousand dollars.

Michael whistled all the way to the terminal. He flashed his brilliant smile and his passport. He took his ticket stub and headed to first class. He sat back and was pleased with himself. Dommie Russell, fat cat of Atlanta, big time business owner and big time thug. Government associate assassin, micro-Mafioso, and small time ghetto hustler from New York to every corner of Atlanta. That kind of acclaim was only mythical before. Women didn't do those things. Yet, his sister was among those ranks. She was as well connected but not as involved with the underworld.

Dommie was sweet and sexy. Part of what Michael said was true and part of it was part of his scheme. He would woo Dommie and get her to tell some of her secrets so that his sister could get a piece of that action. He heard some nasty rumors and he hoped he wouldn't end up swimming with the fishes.

He knows that that is a possibility. He is willing to take the risk. He is a born risk taker. Michael hoped he had made a lasting impression on Dommie and she would request his services again. He knew his sister wouldn't like that but that wasn't for her to decide anymore. Dommie gets what Dommie asks for.

Frederique showed up hoping that he would get lucky. Dommie was fully dressed and having a drink by the pool when he arrived. Frederique had decided to pour out his love for Dommie. He couldn't contain himself any longer. He straightened his tie and rubbed his hand over his bald spot. He had run out of excuses to pay her house calls. At this point, he didn't care about anything. He couldn't sleep and he couldn't eat.

"Okay, what is wrong now Frederique?" Dominiquae was looking at him with her glassy brown eyes. Her eyes followed him from across the pool to the end of her lounge chair.

"May I sit down?"

"No."

Frederique cleared his throat. This was going to be hard. He wasn't sure what would happen but he knew that he would probably live to regret it. "I can't help myself, Dominiquae. I think I have fallen in love with you."

"I think you have lost your job."

"Dommie, do you remember that time we made love?"

"Had sex."

Frederique cleared his voice again. "Didn't you feel anything? I mean, I know I felt that we had made a connection."

That was all she could take. Dominique pulled out the 38 caliber pearl handle and aimed it for his head. She released the safety. "I am going to count to 10 and you had better be out of my sight. 1-2-3-4-10!" Frederique was running towards the exit. She was aiming for his ass but shot a hole in his briefcase instead.

"What the hell is going on down here?" asked Ricki who heard the shots from his room on the fifth floor.

"I had to get rid of that guy. He was becoming annoying. They are no good once they fall in love. His emotions will start to dictate his actions. I can't afford that."

"You know what you're doing. I just don't want you to hit one of the kids by accident, yah know." Ricki was Dommie's younger brother. He was the only one who truly understood her and knew how to talk to her without riling her up.

Instead of flying off the handle, Dommie responded by saying, "I'll be more careful."

Michael's plane lands in San Juan and he looks around for his wife and kids. He doesn't see them. He goes to check out for his one bag and he steps outside. There was nothing like the air in Puerto Rico. All he could smell was the salt sea. He saw his wife pulling up in the white Jeep Cherokee. She was all smiles and the kids were bouncing up and down. Michael never thought about the risk he was taking. He never thought anything could go wrong. What was wrong with a little indiscretion when he could stand to gain so much? His sister is a woman and they tend to worry about nothingness.

"Bueno, bueno! Donde esta me familia?"

"Aqui! Aqui!" The kids sing out in unison. Michael grabs them and hugs them all at once. He loved his kids and he wanted to make sure they had a happy future. He leaned over and kissed Yella. He could smell the hibiscus in her hair and knew he was home.

Yella drove him to his sister's office. JQ was waiting for him. Michael knew he was in for a tongue lashing and he braced himself.

Before he made it through the door good she barked, "I hope you are happy now. You met Dommie and you did what you were supposed to do. Now that's it and I don't want to hear about her anymore. You are not going to be one of her casualties. Men turn up dead in the papers all around her. I will not read about you in the news." Her face was red and she was close to tears. This whole situation was eating her up. "You have a family—my wonderful nieces and nephews. What will happen to them if something happens to you?"

"Dommie will be eating out of my hands." Michael smiled when he thought of the sex.

"My God! My God! You fucking idiot!" JQ was weeping. "Listen, when she calls I will tell her you're dead. You had an accident or something while on vacation." She was hysterical. "What did you do, Mikey? Did you have sex with her?" Michael knew what was coming next. He jumped from the chair and ran to the door. JQ threw the marble horse statue at him. She hit him in the back of his calf. "Get the hell out of here. I mean it!"

JQ knew she had Dommie's business but she didn't want it at the expense of her brother. She knew if Dommie called and asked for Michael again JQ would have to send him to her. She just hoped that he hadn't lied or said anything he'd regret. JQ knew her brother; he lived in a fantasy world sometimes. Dominiquae didn't like liars and she was highly suspicious. This wasn't going to turn out well.

Dommie started thinking about Michael. She wanted to find out about him because he was too enthusiastic. She buzzed Keyba on the intercom. "Can you come down to the lounge. I need a search."

"Sure, Dee." Keyba was in her plush room on the third floor watching Good Times on her 42 inch screen television. She had on her lounging clothes and was consuming a bowl of grapes. She put the bowl on her cherry wood dining table and took her memo pad off of her computer desk. Whenever Dee called, Keyba knew she would have to do some research. She actually loved her job; she just wished Dommie would find a man to take off some of the edge in her voice. On her way down the stairs Keyba remembered that she had invited a male friend over. That fool would have to wait. One thing was for certain, Keyba made sure her male friends and other associates understood the rules of the manor. The raise of an eyebrow could get them and Keyba in a whole heap of trouble.

"Hey girl." Keyba sat in a lounge chair next to Dommie. Dee wasn't untouchable; she just had a lot of pressure on her trying to keep her millions and her associations in line. Dominiquae was a conglomerate. Things blew out of control when she bought some Microsoft stock before the world knew about it. Then, she had invested in Nike. Dommie lucked into the wine business through an associate who needed a loan but couldn't repay her. He turned over all of his assets for a small profit that would sustain him for a few years until he could find a job or come up with some other type of investment. When she saw how easy it was to acquire businesses, she took up all she could in lower Manhattan. Dommie stepped on a few toes because she wouldn't pay for protection. Every day there was a murder or incident with some mob bosses over money and rights. It was ridiculous. Dommie took care of business by involving the Feds. One back scrubs another and before it was all over, she had worked her way into the triangle of the underworld. She cut her loses and moved to Atlanta. She retained some of her assets and made a few friends and a lot more enemies.

"Well, tell me what you think." Keyba was all ears. "I go to a business meeting and I am all about the profit. The guy who is handling the deal works for JQ but I've never seen him before. You know what I do when I get a man in the limo for a few minutes."

"Yep, yep." Keyba nods because she heard the stories. Cunniligus and fellatio were sporting events that took place in the realm of the limo. Dommie had a veracious appetite for male genitalia. It wasn't always pleasant either. One guy left with half a penis. They carried him to the hospital and left him on the sidewalk.

"Any way, this guy is eye candy so there is nothing holding me back from getting an easy high. Do you know what this fool says?"

"What girl, what?" Keyba is leaning on the chair eyes wide open. It was like being in a soap opera.

"He tells me he wants me to get him out of Puerto Rico like they're having a war over there or something. First of all, he flew first class and he has to be a top dog in JQ's company because she kept him away from me for this long and he's not a new chicken. I mean she knows my style, she could have sent him over from day one. The only other thing I know is that he is not very bright. What I want you to do is look him up. His name is Michael Fuentes. If you can't find anything under Fuentes, look under Quinones. I have my suspicions that this muchaho is the golden ram."

Keyba wrote it down. One thing was for sure, Dommie was good. She could figure you out in two minutes. She was blessed with the gift of intuition. All she needed was two minutes in most cases and she'd have your life summed up. Keyba felt bad for the guy. The best thing that could happen now is to get beat up a little. If Dommie said he had three strikes then he was as good as dead. He already had one strike and that was to be suspicious enough to require a search.

JQ was in trouble. She wanted the millions but she didn't want her beloved brother hurt in the process. She knew when she saw him that he had a scheme. He was too confident. You don't come away from a meeting with Dommie smelling like roses unless you had sex with her. Michael was careless. If JQ could smell him when he arrived at the airport, Dommie could smell him too. When she looked out of the window, he strolled up to the building with his tie a loose and that stupid grin on his face like he swallowed a mouse. If Michael had walked up to the building with his tie still in place and the look of a man ready to talk business she would have felt better. She thought long and hard. There was enough history between the two women for JQ to feel comfortable calling Dommie to explain the situation and maybe that would lesson the chance of a fatality. She called her secretary in to fix her a drink. JQ started dialing the US.

It was midnight and Dommie was just finished taking her bath. The phone rang. She knew it had to be someone familiar with her schedule to call at such a time. She answered the phone.

"Buenos noche, hermana. Como esta?"

"Bien, bien. Y tu?" Dommie was glad to talk to JQ. Despite everything, they always remained on good turns. Business was business and that was their philosophy. Only, Dommie knew something was up because JQ was making a personal call. Dommie had a feeling she knew what it was all about.

"I have a problem and a confession." Dommie was silent. "My brother is in over his head and I want you to show him some mercy."

"Is the confession that Michael Fuentes is your brother Michael Quinones and the problem is he may have put himself on a limb?"

"Dommie, he has no idea what he is up against. He's young and foolish."

"I see." Dommie was quiet and that wasn't a good sign. "Jennifer, it was an even worse sign to be called by her first name, "you know the game. You know how I deal with men, brothers, uncles, fathers, and sons. We go back to our days in college when we had nothing together. Remember Jenny?" JQ's heart sank.

From Jennifer to Jenny. It was a black day. Her brother was as good as dead. The ice broke in a split second; typical Dominiquae behavior. "The best thing to do is to head him off. Tell him to stay away from me. That is the only advice I have."

"Are you going to pursue him?" JQ spoke in a whisper.

"Why shouldn't I?"

"He has a wife and kids."

Dommie took that into consideration. "No. I will not pursue him but Jenny, if he crosses my path, he is no longer your brother."

That was fair. JQ could live with that. Dommie kept her promises. JQ just had to make sure that her brother kept his distance. "Te amo, amiga."

"Misma aqui." Dommie drank a glass of wine before she crawled under the covers. The bastard was married. He'd better not cross her path but Dommie knew he would. He had a reason for lying to her and if Dominiquae knew human nature, Michael wasn't going to stop just because his sister warned him against it. Another one bites the dust.

It was six o'clock in the morning and Dommie was sitting at the table eating breakfast in her Victoria's Secret robe. Her cook prepared an old southern dish of apple fritters, cheese grits, toast, and fried fish. Her hair was in place and she sat in the dining area alone. After eating, Dominiquae Russell lit a cigarette and proceeded to stare out of the window. She had five minutes before her bath would be ready and forty minutes before her car would be waiting out front. Every minute of her day was accounted for because she had to keep everyone and every thing in line.

Dommie began to frown when she thought of all the things she would have to accomplish. She had too much to do. This Monday would be highly disappointing. Dommie could feel it in the depths of her being. There was a restlessness and uneasiness in the air.

"Ms. Russell, your bath is ready."

Dommie walked up the one hundred and six flights of stairs to the sixth floor where her bath was and where her clothing was laid out. She always wore a black suit on Mondays. Jonathan bathed her and dressed her. Helena did her hair and made up her face. On her way to the car, her body guards and associates accompanied her. Max, Marcus, X, and Sheila all followed her from the fifth floor. Donna, Train, Lonnie, Jerome, Cal, and Renee followed her from the fourth floor. Kalil, Malik, Fiodora, Donnell, and Keyba followed from the third floor and Monty, Muhammed, Moses, and David from the second. Remus opened her door and Moses, X, Train, and Keyba followed her in.

Each took their glass of Vodka from the table before the limousine pulled off.

"We are short 200 thousand. I called Shorty this morning and she said that money was still coming in but slowly," replied Train.

"Maury said that they had to bust up four people already who were late for their 5 am and 5:30 am drop offs. Between the four there was 50 thousand each," added Moses.

"Two people called in for extensions. Hedda Graham and Davito Manter. They have until next

Monday at 6 at 30% interest compounded daily. They total 200 thousand," said Keyba.

X waited a few minutes before he added his findings to the report. Everyone took sips of vodka and waited. "I found Karla Jisler in England. Terminated. I found Muhammed Elkomy in Saudi Arabia. Terminated. I found Johan Ferna in Switzerland. Terminated. Their assets bring in a total of 781 thousand. It has all been deposited."

"So what you are saying is that we have only 400 thousand over the top?" Dommie was shouting. They knew she was going to have a fit but that was her typical Monday morning style.

"What the fuck am I going to do with 400 thousand, blow my nose? Aghhhhhhh! What?" she screamed as she proceeded to smash the vodka bottle.

"Keyba, you call those mutha fuckers and tell them that they have until tomorrow with 50% interest or they will be floating in a river. X, I want you to find two more deserters by Thursday and wipe their fucking assets clean. Train call Shorty right now and get the figures. Moses, you tell Maury to bust mutha fuckers who are even two seconds late, you got it? I swear if I don't have 600 thousand by Thursday, one of you bastards are gonna disappear foreva. Remus," she screamed, "get these assholes outa here."

"Yes, boss." Remus slammed the breaks. Everyone started scrambling out as Dommie threw the Vodka bottles and glasses. Train shouted out the figures as he fled the flying glass. "We are down by 50 thousand." Dommie eased back in her seat for a few minutes. The figures weren't so bad.

When they pulled up to the office, her hair was a mess, and so was the limousine. She looked in the mirror, put on her hat, and waited for her guards. "Remus, clean up this mess, she muttered as she walked past him. She was all smiles when she walked into the building and saw how busy everyone was. "Good morning, boss" was heard from every direction. Dommie walked into her office alone. She lit a cigarette and gazed out of the window for a minute. So far, nothing unusual but Dommie's gut instincts were always accurate. The phone rang.

"Who the fuck is it Maria? I just sat the fuck down. I didn't even get a chance to look at the figures. It better be fucking important."

"He said his name is Michael Fuentes."

ABOUT THE AUTHOR

Melony Williams was raised in Uniondale, NY. She learned to read early in life and never stopped. Her greatest pleasure came from writing short stories, which she commenced to do at the age of eight. Ms. Williams spent a lot of time developing her writing as an art form. She feels that the ability to write is "man's greatest and most diabolical achievement because of its ability to create and destroy." Her collection of short stories <u>Feminine Hues</u> is about five single women struggling to make their place in the world. Ms. Williams also wrote a collection of short stories called <u>Human Antics</u>, <u>Family Secrets,</u> and <u>A New York Fairy Tale</u>. She also wrote <u>The Serpent Beguiled Me and I Did Eat</u>, which is a religious non-fictional work. Ms. Williams attended Northwood Business Institute in West Palm Beach, Florida and later transferred to the University of Connecticut in Storrs, Connecticut where she graduated in 1992. Ms. Williams currently lives in North Carolina.